C000171090

not yet home

not yet home

JUSTIN CARTWRIGHT

FOURTH ESTATE · London

First published in Great Britain in 1996 by
Fourth Estate Limited
6 Salem Road
London, W2 4BU

A catalogue record for this book is available from the British Library

ISBN 1-85702-403-6

Typeset by Rowland Phototypesetting Ltd,
Bury St Edmunds, Suffolk
Printed in Great Britain by
Clays Ltd, St Ives plc

This book is dedicated to the memory of Solomon T. Plaatje, 1876–1932

The discovery of the plurality of cultures
is never a harmless experience.

Paul Ricoeur

Contents

Foreword

I have travelled widely in South Africa over the last three years, both in the making of a documentary for BBC Television and on behalf of *The Times* and the *Financial Times* newspapers. Being accredited to some prestigious institution helps the inquisitive traveller pursue his interests under the cover of respectability. I am grateful for the camouflage provided.

I would also like to thank Mike and Catrina Popham, Nadine Gordimer, John Karie, Welcome Msomi, Rupert Redesdale, David Rattray, Dan Roberts, Stella Horgan, Mike van Graan and many others for helping me tie up loose ends. And I would like to thank my editor and publisher.

Looking at what I have written, I think I should acknowledge the influence of some of the books I was reading during this period. They include Simon Schama's *Landscape and Memory*; Brian Willian's *Biography of Sol Plaatje*; Johnson and Schlemmer's study of the first democratic election; *The Levinas Reader* edited by Sean Hand; Bruce King's study of Nadine Gordimer's late fiction; Ursula Barnett's *A Vision of Order, A Study of Black South African Literature*. I also acquainted myself reasonably thoroughly with the literature of my native land, something I appeared to know little about at the outset. I interviewed Harold Bloom during this period, and discovered, if I needed reminding, that the notion of culture is never neutral.

Introduction

Martha's Vineyard is quiet. It is as if snow has fallen. This sea mist means that the road to the lighthouse at Gay Head which passes my rented front door is still. This part of the island is anyway not as fashionable or as busy as other parts. We have an Indian Aquinnah just across the road and there are dark, bulky people whom I take to be the Wampanoag, fiddling with their pick-ups or selling lobster rolls or sitting in police cars amiably, not entirely convincing as policemen. These Indians are like stitches in an old garment or almost forgotten appendectomy scars on a body. They are there in among the clapboard holiday homes and the quaint inns and the ice cream parlours as reminders of, and reproaches for, the past, but they are ghostly, as though the substance has been smoked out of them some time ago. This is the country of Moby-Dick; the last man to harpoon a white whale, Amos Smalley, was an Indian from Gay Head.

But I am resisting the temptation to try to unravel the cultural and racial diaspora that has led to present-day Martha's Vineyard, with its Kennedy–Onassis owned beaches, its Indian reservations no larger than small farms, its time-lapsed villages and West Country landscapes. Instead I am reading about the Venda people of the Northern Transvaal in South Africa. It seems they moved from central Africa to their present situation in a series of migrations starting in 1200 and ending in the late seventeenth century. After a century and a half of minding their own business they found themselves in the path of the Boer leader Louis Trichardt, leading his own people away from British control in the South.

I am reading about the Venda because earlier in the year I was filming the Venda snake dance, the *domba*, for a BBC programme on the art and culture of South Africa. At the time it seemed to me that the programme required traditional expressions of culture: the snake dance, I was told, was just that. The truth is that I knew nothing about the snake dance or the Venda other than that the dance is performed by a long conga-line of near-naked girls and that Cyril Ramaphosa, then Secretary-General of the ANC, is a Venda, and therefore unlikely ever to become president. This is how television documentaries are made; slivers of information are quickly worked up into issues of universal concern.

I didn't know then that the Vendas were united under a king called Thoho-yo-Ndou in the late eighteenth century. The main town of Venda, where we were based, is named after this great king. Fifty or sixty years after he had united the Venda, the first white men arrived. There is always a dolorous ring to that phrase. The first white men bring with them, like cholera in a sealed train, the destruction of every society they chance upon. The complexity of their motives, the restless nature of their religion, their urge to own land, their familiarity with guns, the commercial aspect of their lives, all these things entail the end of every society they meet. Now, only a hundred and twenty years later in the case of – to name just two – the Zulu and the Sioux, it seems extraordinary that the white people had such confidence in the superiority of their ways and beliefs. That confidence, evidenced by technological mastery, impressed the people they met too. South Africa's great, forgotten, writer and activist, Solomon Plaatje, describes in his biography of Moroka, the chief of the Bechuana people, the 'tragic friendship' of Moroka's people with the Boers. It was tragic because the Boers quickly forgot Moroka's kindness to them when the threat from more hostile tribes passed. Thirty years later they dispossessed Moroka's people of most of their land, deposed his son and discounted his tribe's beliefs.

Here in Martha's Vineyard, despite lip-service to the eco-friendly lifestyle of Native Americans, there is no more understanding of their former lives. The juggernaut has rolled over these peoples with devastating effect. It may be true, as D.H. Lawrence said in New Mexico, that we have lost the delicate magic of these societies, but the fact is that nobody, not even Native Americans, knows how to put the clock back. What these societies want is to regain the essence of their beliefs, which they now call their 'culture'. The few people who have retained their scepticism about our ways, like the Masai, are fascinating precisely because they have not yet lost the continuity of their culture.

The Venda, once they had come into contact with the Voortrekkers under Louis Trichardt and Hendrik Potgieter, were increasingly subject to the new cosmology. For that is what the white man's arrival entails in all these encounters; it is not just a matter of oppression but of a blinding new vision of the way things work. The Venda tried sporadically to resist. They burnt down early townships and missions. But by the end of the nineteenth century the Boers had caused the chief to flee, and early this century the Venda were completely subjugated and much of their land distributed for white settlement. It's a melancholy tale, but so familiar as to seem preordained. With the loss of sovereignty comes a loss of culture, or at least a severe diminution of identity. If the local customs are not proof against the white man, what chance has the culture of surviving?

In South Africa today, the search is on for the submerged or denigrated cultures, ground under in the past hundred years. This raises tricky questions about the relative merits of cultures. It leads to absurdities in the attempts to redress the balance; it causes otherwise sensible people to believe that culture forged in the 'struggle' is essentially more valuable than bourgeois culture. Nonetheless there is a laudable impulse to discover some value in the diversity of culture. Perhaps inevitably, culture has become a catchall for everything which is neither political nor oppressive, when in truth all cultures have always been in competition.

As I read about the Venda I see that they have one of the longest histories of iron-smelting in Africa. This sort of fact is always cited to counter the idea that Africans were living in a state of sloth and ignorance when the white people found them. Indeed the Venda do appear to have had thriving tool-making, textile and pottery manufactures. But it was largely downhill from the moment their land was reapportioned, and catastrophic when they were invited to believe they were an independent nation by the National Party government.

By the time of the recent elections in South Africa, the Venda were deeply divided. One of the most contentious subjects was the poisoning of political rivals. The newly independent Venda had set up institutions and a defence force which in reality gave power and wealth to those who went along with the government in Pretoria. Traditional practices, like the snake dance, have become associated in some people's minds with corruption and Uncle Tomism. In 1988 there was a school boycott and a widespread strike. Part of the cause of this unrest was a medicine murder. A young girl was murdered and parts of her body were removed, including her head, a hand, a leg, genitals and her tongue. A man was arrested who testified that he had been promised payment by the father of the deceased. He named names. The father and other suspects were arrested, but the case was dismissed. The case was re-opened after protest; again the charges were dismissed. This led to public outrage. There were seventeen other cases of apparent ritual murder during the year. Ritual murder had become a political issue, the implication being that the reactionaries were using it for political ends. The Youth Movement took the lead in denouncing the murders. The Youth Movement, which thinks of itself as the ANC on the ground, has come, apparently, to dominate traditional 'structures'. ('Structures' is a word which has entered the vocabulary of the new South Africa in a big way.)

And as I sit here in the mist, I see that the political and cultural complexity of South Africa has been masked by the more obvious struggle. The proof of this complexity, if it is needed, is that a group of youths marching back from the rally to celebrate Nelson Mandela's release in 1990 stoned a 'witch' to death and burned her body. In another expression of the new political realities, nine suspected witches were burned in one night.

So it seems that as we made our way to the *domba* dance, I was almost criminally unprepared for the task of filming which lay ahead. The *domba* ritual is one of three that Venda girls undergo to prepare themselves for womanhood. The dance is only one aspect of a long process, not the whole thing, as I probably imagined. But as I read my study of the Venda and their customs, I wonder how many different rituals there are, how many tribes and peoples and clans, all struggling with the expectation of the new South Africa, yet still encumbered with the beliefs and traditions of the recent past. I wonder, too, if any accommodation can ever be made between the flickering, firelit past and the new, neon, society. Probably only by reducing their complexity and the perverseness of their culture (I am using the word now) to pabulum.

Up the road from me here in Martha's Vineyard is a store which sells, among many things, medicine-man blankets. It turns out they are manufactured in a factory to a pattern used by the Indians of the Pacific West, five thousand miles from here. This is probably the way it will go in South Africa: the dances, the imprecations, the artefacts, the songs, will all be milled down to a bland and acceptable culture. In fact this has already started. At Nelson Mandela's inauguration, three hundred *sangomas* – the traditional healers, formerly known as witch-doctors – were invited on stage to lend colour to the ceremony. At the opening ceremonies of the Rugby World Cup last year, hundreds of non-specific African dancers were choreographed in a relentlessly colourful process of trivialisation.

Our first attempt to film the snake dance was a let-down. We drove up a track some miles though patches of mealies and scattered huts, to find the spot our guide, a cheerful girl who was planning to be a social worker ('I am very social and a hard worker') said was the meeting-point for our prearranged dance. Something was wrong. The dancers were in an advanced stage of middle age. It was not easy to explain or justify the fact that we wanted lissom, naked girls rather than elderly women, however true to the tradition of the *domba* their movements might be. I had the uncomfortable feeling that we had asked the Women's Institute to get dressed up in their gymslips. A boy of about eleven was in tears. I asked why. It seemed he should have been playing for his football team and was not happy to be dressed in scratchy skins banging a drum.

For all the makeshift quality of the event, it was moving. Two huge drums, carved with elephant heads, were used and a kudu horn was blown to assemble our participants (in reality hiding just out of sight for the purposes of the filming). Our embryonic social worker took part; she was by far the youngest participant and yet she had done her initiation five years before, when she was fifteen. It seemed to me essential to try to film the real thing. It turned out by good fortune that a genuine *domba* was taking place that evening not many miles away. I heard myself asking, 'How many virgins can we find by five o'clock?'

We found the village and I entered negotiations with the headman. At first it was a question of dealing with him through his sons, one of whom was very drunk on homebrew, which he offered me in a wooden ladle. There was a certain amount of pretence that the issue of filming the *domba* had to be widely discussed, with emissaries sent higher up the hierarchical chain. (I read that the Venda are a very hierarchical people, with a number of aristocratic families ruling the roost. But I don't know what this means.) From the start, however, it was simply a question of money. When it was established that we were prepared to pay, the headman appeared. He and I sat in his neat, mud-walled courtyard; one of his wives approached on her knees and crouched near him on the baked cow-dung floor. The three sons sat on a narrow decorative ledge of mud which abutted one of the huts. The Venda and other people in the area are known for the decoration of their homesteads. The painting is bold and geometric, like middle Picasso. We settled on a figure of about fifty pounds, which, I think, was probably far more than they were expecting. From then on there was no talk of higher authority. We were bidden to come back at four or five. There would be at least thirty virgins.

The authentic *domba*, which I now know is one of a series of rites that young girls pass through, took place as the sun was setting. It started around the base of a large tree about a quarter of a mile from the headman's village. The headman himself, in Panama hat and mustard-yellow sports coat, was on hand to lend his expertise. He was keen that the dance should process through a new building, almost finished, on the edge of his property, and was busy placing a cement bag as a temporary step up to make access possible. The young girls assembled. They wore very small skirts, for modesty purposes only, some bead jewellery, and coloured pieces of cloth attached to their upper arms. They were friendly, not at all embarrassed by their nakedness. Under the direction of an older woman, one of the headman's wives, they began their stylised rhythm. It was beautiful to watch as the girls moved in a sensuous, undulating circle, linked tightly together to the beat of the drums. These drums, I noticed, were not as well cared for as the drums we had seen earlier, but they too were decorated with elephant heads and crocodile shapes. The elephant and the crocodile are Venda totemic beasts.

The movements were certainly evocative of a python, but also of a Polynesian canoe being paddled by an all-girl crew, everybody dipping and pulling in time. This went on for more than an hour, first from the starting point around the tree and then up to the headman's village. A much older man, wearing a little coronet of cowhide and a thin calico robe, walked with the girls. He carried a small whip, which occasionally he pretended to use on the girls to encourage them. It was growing dark. The fire glowed in the centre of the village. A strange thing happened: in the middle of one of the dances the girls lay down in an unmistakable attitude of sexual surrender, but still attached like a paperchain.

I read now that the very obvious fertility and sexual connotations of the dance were not just in my mind. The drum represents the womb and jumping on the drum and straddling it 'represents intercourse'. What does 'represent' mean in this context? As anyone who has tried to speak a foreign language idiomatically knows, there's a disproportionate amount of importance lurking in the nuances and subtleties. The male organ is apparently often referred to as the 'pole' or 'tree'. A line of one of the accompanying songs goes: 'The grass rustles as the falling tree parts it.' How do we know how lightly this is taken? Is it playful, or ironic or deadly serious? As I read now about Venda initiation rites I wonder if the anthropological way of looking at these things really tells the whole story.

Now the girls became more animated: they were released from their conga line but continued to dance for the fun of it. They wanted to stroke the long hair of the production manager. They wanted us to take their photographs. We parted with affection, I thought. I was eager to say goodbye to the headman, but he had vanished. From his hut came a message that he was lying down, perhaps recovering from the excitement of the python dance. We drove away into the woodsmoke-scented night reluctantly, certain that we would never again see these people.

Now, many months later, Martha's Vineyard is stunned by the sea mist into silence. This morning, in an encyclopedia of Native Americans, I read that the Wampanoag tribe is extinct. Yet across the road is their Aquinnah, or community centre. The tribe must have reinvented itself out of the apocalypse which struck the American Indian people, when tribes were lumped together or exterminated altogether. I can't, however, take that one any further. At the moment I am wrestling with the notion of the new South Africa, a country which, like the Wampanoag, has reinvented itself.

The past few years have been described by my friend Frederik van Zyl Slabbert, once leader of the Progressive Party, as 'deal-driven'. Slabbert is fond of this kind of academic jargon; what he means is that a deal has been struck by those in possession of the material wealth and expertise and those in command of the political numbers. Some years ago, long before Mandela was released, Slabbert told me that the two sides would have to get together one day; neither could make headway without the other. At the time I thought that this probably gave too much weight to the importance of the whites in any possible political settlement, but he has been proved right, as he has about most things.

There may have been a deal struck between the National Party and the ANC, but there are many more accommodations to be made, which have nothing to do with political power but everything to do with the human experience. The startling diversity and unfamiliarity of South Africa have been masked for many years. The new South Africa is, as this excursion to Venda showed me, a country where those who grew up there now realise that they were living in a dream of passing strangeness.

PART I

1994

Chapter 1

Nadine Gordimer's house is in Frere Road, Parktown, a leafy and quite old-fashioned suburb of Johannesburg. Further north, the suburbs have taken on a jaunty Mediterranean–Californian look, with plenty of terracotta tiles and banana trees and fancy driveways. But in Parktown you still see the English suburban outlines. Two streets below Frere is Barkly Road, and that is where I lived between the ages of fifteen and twenty, when I left for England. Even in those days, the very early sixties, Nadine Gordimer loomed over South African literature. Down below in Barkly Road, as schoolboy and then student, harbouring ambitions to write, I felt the penumbra cast on to our modest twenties house.

In 1994 I met her for the first time to discuss filming her for the BBC. I had recently reviewed *My Son's Story* with lukewarm praise and I had spoken about her on radio at the time of her Nobel prize in rather qualified terms; cravenly I hoped she would have no idea of who I was. I was early, naturally, and drove around the suburb I had not seen since 1965. Our old house had been smartened up, disguising its simple but comfortable origins. I located my bedroom where I used to swing from the door-jamb to build up my chest and where I once wrote an absurdist play in three days. My father, who was a notoriously impractical man, calculated that every bath I took (long and introspective) was costing him 14/6d, about £11 in today's money. Later he redid his calculation and discovered that it was costing him 1.4 pence. He was editor of the *Rand Daily Mail* at the time.

Nearby was a house where a distinguished academic was said to have shot five burglars over the years. Maybe he attracted burglars, because we never had one, and as far as I can remember had no precautions against them. But now I noticed that almost every house was directly linked to an 'armed response'. I have read that nearly 200,000 people are employed in private security firms in the Johannesburg region. Nadine Gordimer has armed response. Other houses in Frere Road have topped off their walls with razor wire and electric filaments. Johannesburg was rife with stories of robbery, hijacking and murder. There always had been murder and robbery, but largely localised in the black areas from where it was commonplace to hear rumours of servants being murdered and gangsters shooting up shebeens. At a safe distance it sounded quite exciting. The city centre and the suburbs were comparatively Arcadian, and strangely quiet at night when all the black people were obliged to go home.

Johannesburg now is a very different city. Every street corner has become a makeshift market – known as 'the informal economy' – and every residential block a crowded slum. Most visitors loathe Johannesburg. It's true that on first acquaintance it has little to recommend it, but to those of us who were brought up there, and to most of South Africa's black leadership, it has an inexplicable charm. The university, where I passed three lively years, is not far from Nadine Gordimer's house. It is one of the ugliest campuses in the world. The city itself is a cut-price version of Denver or LA. The countryside around is clapped out, completely featureless, and the townships are huge, sprawling and dangerous. Yet it is a lively, stimulating place. In 1995 the opening night of the Zulu *Macbeth*, as audience and cast spilled into the foyer of the Civic Theatre, was an extraordinary spectacle and could only have happened in Johannesburg. Wildly overdressed society women mingled with Zulus in leopard-skins, and the arts community in unspeakable Zaïrean suits of lights mingled with the old Anglos in dinner-jackets.

It is not unusual for South Africans to say that they can't read Nadine Gordimer. Yet I found from an early age that her writing was not only readable but inescapably influential. All South African writers who have followed seem to me to be under her spell to some degree, even Coetzee and Hope. For me, the Gordimer of *The Conservationist* and the short stories was impressive, but at the same time too restrictive. Harold Bloom said to me of John Updike: 'Minor novelist with major style.' (I don't agree.) But it makes me wonder if in some way it is possible for the style, and in Gordimer's case the strength of mind, to be stronger than the narrative and wordsmithing talent.

She had passed seventy in 1994 and I was prepared for a little decay. I was also expecting a much larger, more obviously forceful person. When she opened the door, I was struck first by how small she is and secondly by how beautiful. At seventy she has a lively interest and commitment. As I was to find out, and as I suspect Reinhold, her husband, has long since accepted, Nadine Gordimer is never going to be sitting quietly knitting the grandchildren's bootees and exchanging domestic platitudes. From the moment I met her I was captivated. Somehow my feelings about her books have changed as a result. I had thought *My Son's Story* a little contrived, perhaps even wooden; I realised that the themes of sexual betrayal and familial loneliness are not the work of an isolated, elderly writer, but deeply felt, and, in some way I am not privy to, based on personal experience. Her more recent book, *None to Accompany Me*, I take to be even more intensely personal. It is also at least as good as her work of twenty years ago.

A Nobel laureate – the first I have met – is nonetheless awe-inspiring. But her house, by Herbert Baker, I found immediately familiar. Indeed for a brief period we also lived in a Baker house not far away. My visits to South Africa over the past two years have been for me a series of landscapes evocatively recalled. There are moments in South Africa when violent lightning storms illuminate the landscape, so that for an instant everything is strikingly caught as in a photograph by Helmut Newton. This house, I realised, reminded me powerfully and unbidden of my own childhood. In my writing I am often as powerfully drawn to the places as the people of my childhood.

Gordimer and I talked about the filming I was preparing and the future role of 'white writing'. She denied that there was really such a thing. In a sense she is right: white South Africans are certainly not Europeans, as the signs on the bus shelters once proclaimed: EUROPEANS ONLY. There are, too, points where their lives meet those of Africans. But white South Africans, particularly white writers, are above all concerned with their whiteness in an African world. Gordimer said many years ago, 'First you leave your mother's house and later you leave the home of the white race.' You may well leave its prejudices, but you don't become an African by doing so. It has been the singular advantage of South African writers to express the white viewpoint because, of course, the liberal predicament in South Africa was an exciting and clear-cut version of the liberal predicament everywhere. And Gordimer's particular strength has been her constant examination of the white woman in South Africa.

The drawing room at Gordimer's house has some lovely paintings. A Toulouse-Lautrec chalk, a Degas, bronze heads, some African art. The *New York Review of Books* is on display and down the corridor two servants are occasionally visible. Gordimer was busy because the election was only a few months off. She is a fervent supporter of the ANC and did not rise to my diffident suggestion that writers who express any political preferences usually live to regret it. The ANC was, and probably still is, much more than a political party. This led to resentment amongst those in the arts who thought that the ANC was introducing cultural commissars to support the large philosophic claims of the ANC. Mongane Wally Serote, the chairman of the ANC's Arts Panel, was cited as the worst of these commissars. Serote is a good poet and a close friend of Gordimer's, who has lived many years in exile. Gordimer could see no problems on the horizon. Of course there had been misjudgements, and of course the nature of the democracy had been obscured in some quarters in the euphoria. Negotiations were going on in many areas of public life, including the arts. I was to discover just how true this was: South Africa has become the negotiating capital of the world in the last few years. A blizzard of papers and documents has rained down on the country. It had occurred to me as I attended the all-party talks at Kempton Park earlier in the year that the process of negotiation itself was probably the single greatest seminar in democracy undertaken anywhere in recent history.

Gordimer said that she had been active in ANC voter education programmes. There was a long way to go; even with elections coming soon, many rural people hadn't got a clue. She had also been negotiating with the Performing Arts Councils, the traditional recipients of governmental arts funding, which owned large theatres in major cities and supported ballet and opera. Late in the day they had realised that change was on the way and were now struggling to find a new role. They were trying to co-opt black people, and somehow imagined they would still be in charge of their own destiny. Gordimer told me, scornfully, that they had just staged *The Merry Widow* in Pretoria; she made it sound like a reading of *Mein Kampf*.

I was strangely eager to blow my own cover. I felt uncomfortable, as though I were pulling some sort of confidence trick. I wanted to say, 'Look, Nadine, I'm not really from the BBC, I'm Justin from down there in Barkly Road, and my father's name was Paddy. You probably knew him.' But I sat there instead, a stuffed chicken, talking about culture in South Africa, like a disinterested and quite well-informed outsider. Melding of the cultures had already taken place, she said. Albie Sachs, an ANC returnee who had lost an arm to a bomb in Lourenço Marques, had earlier suggested that a new spring of culture was needed, a joyous upsurge. She felt the theatre, and particularly the Market, was one area where a new and significant culture could be seen emerging. She told me that she had once contemplated moving to central Africa for a while, but she realised that there she would be seen as a European, whereas here she was accepted, the only place where she was unequivocally herself, although she loved Britain and the English language had shaped her.

Gordimer's house was spare, spacious, comfortable and tasteful. I thought, as I sat there, how different it was from the homes of Africans, however eminent, that I have seen, which favour grey leather-look lounge suites and knick-knacks and coloured glass. Are taste and culture different? Is culture an expression of taste, and in that sense, personal identity? In the excruciatingly nuanced middle-class world of England with which I have become familiar, the question of social gradation buzzes like a fly trapped in a bottle. But here there were bigger issues than taste. Gordimer has always taken some satisfaction in the idea that you can't make omelettes without breaking eggs. When she described feminist issues as 'piffling', she meant of course, feminism in South Africa as contrasted with deprivation and racial prejudice. A year later, when I asked her about the issue that was then exercising English-speaking South Africans, the botched attempt to make radio in some fashion mirror the aspirations of society, she agreed that the English language was being murdered. But, she said, falling standards for the minority were to be expected, even welcomed, because they would of course be accompanied by rising standards for the majority. I could hear the eggs being smashed.

Here in Frere Road, nicely poised above Barkly Road, there was no sign of falling standards. Somebody at the BBC had suggested I call my programme 'Nadine Gordimer's Swimming Pool'. There was no swimming pool, but the garden, like every aspect of Gordimer's life, is nicely judged, pleasant without being huge, just as the house is comfortable without being ostentatious.

I felt envious in a way. Her writing is firmly tied to place (although she has ventured out into Africa), and her career has fallen very neatly into the period of apartheid. She has always followed the story closely and tried to keep ahead. *My Son's Story*, I thought, showed too obviously, by having a coloured family as its subject, her realisation that the new South Africa was going to turn away from the political as its main motive force. Perhaps too, I thought, she was thinking about her own career: she may not have wanted to be too closely allied to the narrative of history. She has pointed out, and I agree with her, that history is often far better portrayed by novelists than by historians ('Nothing I say here will be as true as my novels'). There can be no doubt at all that few novelists have given a truer or more telling account of their times than Nadine Gordimer. But perhaps she had wondered if novel-writing were not just a part of the historical process; as they say in South Africa, part of the problem rather than the solution. Her reaction might be to lay weight on the sexual and familial tensions out of which artistic endeavour and political involvement are born. This is a lonely task, essentially inexplicable either in Freudian or in Marxist terms, but it is one that Gordimer has taken on without flinching. In *July's People*, Maureen at the end is 'like a solitary animal . . . existing only for their lone survival'. In her most recent work, *None to Accompany Me*, Vera Stark, who is closest of all her characters to being a fictional *alter ego*, almost rejoices in her aloneness. I now see that this is the greatness of her writing, the single-mindedness of her study of the individual will and predicament.

A month later, on election day, 1994, Gordimer was wearing a Nelson Mandela button. She was in a lively mood, nervous and elated. It was her first election, she said, although she had voted before. All over South Africa people were elated by the chance to vote. We had already been to Alexandra Township and filmed the lines of people, stretching for hundreds of yards, wanting to vote. There had been some anxiety among the crew. We were forbidden to enter a township by our insurance policy. One English member of the crew wanted to keep the engine running for a quick getaway. I walked with Jon, the cameraman, down an endless line of cheerful and excited people, congratulating myself on my courage until we came upon a Dutch television crew moving in the opposite direction. We exchanged fraternal greetings. The mood of Alexandra, which is a nasty place, a spill of shanties and rubbish and open drains, not far from the most prosperous suburbs in South Africa, was happy and expectant. The lines shuffled patiently forward. It was as if they were waiting at the bank for a payment which would be instant.

Gordimer was canvassing support near to home, she said, at the polling station at the Anglican church. Polling day produced its own myths: an elderly couple confronted by the long lines left their cook in place while they went out to lunch. An MP, Peter Soal, told me that another couple, arriving with their servants in the back of the Mercedes, inquired where the maids were to vote. In Natal, an arrangement was being made: David Steel, the chief observer, said to me that he had presided over a free and fair fraud there. I wondered if Gordimer felt, like so many dissidents in eastern Europe, regret at the passing of the old order which had provided almost risibly unambiguous moral superiority for those in opposition. No, she said that this was the most exciting day of her life. But I wondered, and I wonder still, if there isn't a dreadful letdown in store for the liberal whites as they realise something which was obscured by apartheid, that all political endeavour brings disillusionment. That politics casts a retrospective gloom.

We filmed her paintings and bronzes before she came in, and we filmed her reading from *None to Accompany Me.* South Africans reading aloud have, of course, a memory of standard English, but it competes with a relentless monotone, underscoring it like cicadas on a hot day. Afrikaans South Africans and African South Africans often speak English with more conviction, in the same way that Welsh and Irish bring more richness to the task. On the second reading, done for close-up, she read with some emotion. But South Africa is not an articulate country, and the spoken word, as in America, is being winnowed, to leave strictly functional material.

Gordimer had been asked to read at the President's inauguration, scheduled for a month's time. I wanted to know what she would read. I could imagine this small figure, not widely loved or read in South Africa, standing up there reading to a largely indifferent audience. I feared for her. She was going to read from *None to Accompany Me*. We discussed the true significance of the first election and the question of language and culture. Underlying my questions, I now realise, was the urge to find out if she was prepared to be disillusioned by the new South Africa. There is an almost impossible contradiction between a writer who at heart is sceptical and aware of ambiguity, and membership of a political party. But for Gordimer the ANC is a philosophical movement too. It has been the agent of all she has been hoping for. In her support for COSAW, the Congress of South African Writers, I see the attempt to bring the coherence of her views to a corner of the political struggle. Although Gordimer says that there are promising black writers in South Africa, nobody so far has broken out. There is no new Plaatje or Richard Rive or Bessie Head. Some of the street poetry and protest writings are lamentable. But it must be true, from Gordimer's point of view, that encouraging black writers is going to yield results. It is only by the triumph of black leaders and black vision that the circle can be squared.

Gordimer is only a few years younger than Mandela. It's taken a very long time but, I thought, there must be great satisfaction in seeing not only her ideas and convictions, but also those of her peers, triumph in this way. Because it is the generation of people who have been in the struggle almost from the start of apartheid proper who have triumphed. And they are the direct heirs of Albert Luthuli and Sol Plaatje, educated men who believed in amelioration and gradualism. Albert Luthuli actually stayed with Gordimer during his trial in the fifties. The real start of apartheid, Gordimer agreed, was in 1913 with the Natives Land Act, just about the time the Venda were finally seeing the way the future looked. But the Nationalist government of 1948 was the formal beginning of what the world recognised as apartheid. Mandela and Gordimer have a friendship which goes back a long way. I naturally wondered, without articulating the thought, if they had ever been lovers. Later Gordimer was to tell me of going round to Mandela's mansion in Houghton for tea. The maid – dressed in a *doek*, she said, and slip-slopping along – served them two cups of tea with the tea bags still in them. Gordimer was amused but also upset that this is how the President lives. At the time of the election the split with Winnie was complete, but the damage to his inner self, if it can be measured by the letters he wrote to Winnie from Robben Island and Pollsmoor, must be extensive. Gordimer confirmed this. And at his divorce hearing he described his loneliness.

There is another aspect of South African life which struck me: in a country which is poorly educated, with a staggeringly banal level of popular discourse, there are some towering figures and three or four of them have received Nobel prizes, including Gordimer. Somehow the liberal, democratic tendency has won through in every political forum including the arts. There was a suspicion that whites had manipulated the process; I now think, two years on, that it is Mandela's authority and the support of the other heavyweights, including Gordimer, that has given the process its stability. But it seems to be an inescapable fact that all these people, with the exception of De Klerk, have sprung from a traditional, Anglocentric education.

I was to attend many hours of debate and to talk to a large number of people involved in the question of arts funding. At this stage – the election of 1994 – there was still a feeling that the ANC's commissars would seek to control the arts as they had to some extent in the lead-up to the transitional period. During that debate, there was very little discussion of education; instead, an emphasis was placed on structures and 'funding and community initiatives' and so on. It was also clear throughout that 'whites unfortunately have the habit of taking over and usurping the leadership and taking the crucial decisions', as Desmond Tutu has said. Serote, the supposed red under the cultural bed, wrote, 'Blacks must learn to talk, whites must learn to listen.'

After we had spoken, Gordimer was keen to be off to the polling station. She disappeared to the kitchen and re-emerged with a sandwich, which she began to eat hurriedly on the stoep. Reinhold Cassirer, her husband, who is more obviously elderly, fussed around, suggesting she comb her hair. She refused. He smiled indulgently. And then she was off, still nibbling her sandwich, in an old Volvo, to the polling station. Cars, as is well known, tell you a lot about their owners. This one is from the period before Volvo pulled out of South Africa. It's a car that speaks of seriousness and modesty, but also a certain amount of calculation about appearances.

She has written that the white person in South Africa does not know, as the black knows, that he will be home at last. And yet there she was, in her elderly car, going up the road to the polling station, not to secure a home for the whites, but to serve the logic of all she has written. She has decided, simply, that culture must be allied to the political struggle to validate it, as much as she protests that her writing is separate from her activities as a citizen.

For myself, I hold to the view of Milan Kundera, speaking of Robert Musil, that culture should be protected from the mindlessness of politics. But when, at the age of twenty, I left 6 Barkly Road and the long shadow cast by Nadine Gordimer I turned my back on the struggle.

Chapter 2

I arranged to meet Welcome Msomi. 'Welcome' is the sort of name which comes from the mission-school era. In my youth, black people had no names other than these cheerful or solemnly biblical names. To this day I doubt that most white people know their servants' family names. Welcome Msomi may come equipped with an anachronistic name, but in his career he gives a pointer to the future of South Africa. Although he is close to the ANC leadership, he is not a card-carrying member. He has embraced the worlds of public relations and the musical theatre enthusiastically and with success.

Nadine Gordimer had suggested I talk to him because he was organising the inauguration of the new president, to be held nearly three weeks after the election. He had devised a slogan, 'One nation, many cultures', which had already been traduced in some circles to 'Many nations, no culture'. It seemed to me a good opportunity to see how culture was to be regarded in the new South Africa, although I had already become aware that little thought had been given to the nature of culture. Certainly nobody was sticking his neck out to claim that there was a higher culture, achieved not through slogans and good intentions, but through self-improvement or education. In fact any notion of a higher culture was, I realised, considered undemocratic at this moment, because history was thought to have taken a deeply significant turn in South Africa. We were thought to be servants of that history, required to pay our respects; this was certainly not the moment to ask questions about the true nature of culture.

Yet, as Van Zyl Slabbert said, this moment in history came about because the people with the money and the people with the numbers got together. You would have to be a very unusual determinist to believe that the grand designs of history work in this way, the way of liberal democracy, the compromise and the pragmatic elevated to a matter of principle. It is Mandela who has brought an element of the mythical and fantastical to South Africa. He is an embodiment of the transfiguration of South Africa, the prisoner become president. It is almost sacramental. F.W. de Klerk is left looking as though he is made of far more earthy materials, while Mandela has floated above politics in a way that is unique in modern times. And his great prestige has been applied to the notion that higher nationhood can embrace all South Africans, whatever their differences. The fact that the election showed clearly that the minorities were shrewdly assessing their best options under the new system casts doubt on this hope, but it was certainly true that there was an immense pride in the standing of the new South Africa, which derived largely from Mandela, but also from the prosaic presence of F.W. de Klerk. Mandela and the ANC, I had been warned by Breyten Breytenbach, are tough, ruthless and manipulative. There were occasionally glints in Mandela of the iron-willed revolutionary, as when he faced Buthelezi's reluctance to join in the election.

In those weeks I had a sense of the fragility of the body politic as the election approached. This sense was enhanced by a massive explosion in Johannesburg. I visited the site of the bomb with Albie Sachs, to film him there as – I thought – a reminder of what had happened to him in Mozambique when he lost an arm and was blinded in one eye. It was possible that this bomb was placed by the same people, former members of the same organisation as the one in Mozambique. Johannesburg was tense. Young white soldiers patrolled the area anxiously. It was early winter in South Africa and in the cold evening the devastation of the streets, the razor wire rolled out from the brutal army vehicles, suggested a future which was chaotic and dangerous. I thought that evening that civil society would break down. Albie walked past the razor wire for the camera, his lack of an arm a badge of distinction. Behind him some youths were moving furniture away from the scene of the blast. Nobody greeted Albie or appeared to know who he was. I had then an inkling of the disappointment and even sorrow that he experienced on his return to South Africa. Imagine: you have been imprisoned, you have worked tirelessly for a revolutionary future, you have had your prison diaries dramatised by the National Theatre, you have lost an eye and an arm in an explosion set by the security forces, and you can walk down a Johannesburg street unrecognised. At that moment the possibility of one nation seemed to be a cruel deception.

Yet that night I attended a choral concert in the City Hall, not many blocks from the explosion, a programme of traditional songs with audience participation, conducted by Richard Cock and James Khumalo. I had been told that no white people dared go into the town after dark any more, but there was a full house, largely of whites thirsty for some spiritual refreshment and desperate to applaud the arrangements of James Khumalo and his Soweto Songsters. I discussed with Sandile Khemese, the leader of the Soweto String Quartet, one of the violinists, the future of classical music in South Africa, and he said that black South Africans were keen to learn and to take part. He regretted that his own training had been inadequate because of apartheid. It made him bitter but he could forgive.

Richard Cock, the manager of the National Symphony Orchestra, was, I discovered, at the same school as me. He carries in his wallet a picture of Dr Claude Brown, our music teacher and choirmaster. Cock's orchestra is funded by the SABC and this use of money was already the target of some sniping. The composition of the orchestra has also been under attack. Not only is it almost exclusively white, but the majority of its members are not even South African. There seems to be a lively trade in wind and string players from the Balkans and from the former Eastern bloc.

Richard Cock conducted the orchestra with the sort of fervour and informality you would associate with the Proms. He made plenty of corny jokes. After the concert I spoke to Cock and Professor James Khumalo, the conductor of the Soweto Songsters, who took a very prominent part in the concert. Khumalo believed that the orchestra should be Africanised with all possible speed. The evidence that the Soweto Songsters could bring something uniquely African to choral singing was overwhelming: they sang a Welsh hymn in Sotho, and some other arrangements of traditional music. The audience, largely white, was entranced, sensing that there was some hope in this shared love of music. Khumalo was able to announce that Buthelezi would take part in the elections after all, something we all knew by then, but it gave added comfort to the audience, which was looking for scraps of assurance about the future as well as enjoying the traditional spiritual buffet on offer.

Later I filmed Sandile Khemese in his small neat house in Soweto, practising, while his young children played blithely outside, and I saw yet again what should have been obvious: South Africans of every colour were trying to get on with their lives. It was not a very surprising revelation, but it chimed with what Desmond Tutu had said: expectations are not wildly extravagant. In the fickleness of my emotions, I felt my unworthy doubts dissolving.

Welcome Msomi is a Zulu. He produced the Zulu *Macbeth*, *Umabatha*, in the sixties and took it to Europe and then to America. His wife, Thuli Dumakude, played Lady Macbeth in the original production and he played Duncan (Dingane). He worked both in theatre and in public relations for a drug company. As I was to discover, he and his wife are a powerful team. Welcome had been given the task of organising the inauguration and some other events such as Mandela's birthday party in 1994. An advertising agency in Johannesburg had set up a new company, of which he was now managing director, to produce events. Meeting Msomi in one of those pastel-shaded, leanly-equipped offices which advertising agencies favour, I asked him about his background. He was educated first at St Christopher's School in Swaziland, from where finally he applied to the University of Natal in 1964, but his application was blocked by the government. He started his own theatre company and eventually, after extraordinary adventures escaping his creditors and enemies, a reviewer was persuaded to come and see his first production. This led to the offer of some space at the university and the production of *Macbeth* which launched him and his Zulu Dance Theatre. The Zulu *Macbeth* toured the world and he and his wife Thuli ended up in New York in the eighties. Thuli had starred in *Poppie Nongema*, which I remembered seeing at Hammersmith. It's the only time I've been to a play and seen every single member of the audience in tears. Anyway, in 1990 Mandela called. They met and Msomi returned to South Africa. Like Lloyd George, Mandela seems to have known an enormous amount of people.

Msomi, like many Africans, dresses more formally than his white counterpart would. At first he seemed to be more PR than musical producer, but I soon discovered that he had ambitious plans for the inauguration. The elections and the transitional arrangements, including a secret deal to transfer thousand of hectares to the Zulu king, were costing the exchequer millions of rands, so I could imagine that Pretoria was powerless to resist Msomi's lavish plans. These plans included readings from South Africa's writers, a huge choir, *sangomas* (the traditional medicine men and women), African music, Indian music, ballet, opera, rock, jazz and *boeremusiek* (the traditional Afrikaans farmer's music), and the participation of some of South Africa's six orchestras. Above all, Msomi wanted contributions from every region and every racial group. For him it was clear that culture could be used to express the notion, the one by which the ANC lived, that there was a transcendent South African identity. This identity had, of course, been suppressed by apartheid. Apartheid was contrary to the African spirit of *ubuntu*, humanity, which I was beginning to hear more of. It was as if one grand notion like apartheid had been toppled by another which was moving to fill the vacated space. It seemed to be difficult for the many Marxists in the ANC and in the universities to accept that there might be no dialectic in history. Yet Msomi, I thought, was ideally equipped to bring the notion of one nation to the masses in a recognisable form.

He planned to use all the terraces sweeping down from the Union Buildings for his show. Herbert Baker, him again, had designed the Union Buildings to bring some imperial dignity to the little dusty town of Pretoria. I had been there to meet Pik Botha a few years before, as David Steel's advisor. It is now known that the government had been negotiating with Mandela indirectly for years, since the beginning of the eighties, but Botha, from his spacious office looking down on to the same gardens where Msomi now proposed to stage his inauguration fiesta, gave no indication. Indeed, he asked, 'Why are you people always talking about this Mr Mandela? There are other leaders in South Africa, you know. And Mr Mandela has no experience of government or press conferences or running anything.' We were too stunned to point out that his government had kept Mandela in jail for the previous twenty-three years. I see now that perhaps the argument in Cabinet had been about how competent Mandela would be, and how quickly the country would revert to the Stone Age if he were given any power. But at the time it seemed a bizarre remark. Botha has always appeared to me to be the Boris Yeltsin of South African politics, lacking only the mad courage.

Msomi told me that he was inviting Nico Carstens, a player of *boeremusiek*, and Ray Phiri, Africa's own authentic rock star. Carstens had a hit in the early sixties called 'Zambezi', played on his accordion, and Phiri was the man behind the

African sound of Paul Simon's *Graceland*. Phiri and Carstens had apparently formed a close relationship; they were working on a fusion of their music. Msomi gave me the impression that one of the ways forward for South Africa was an actual fusion of musical styles of performance. He believed it could be done with the national anthem, and he also believed that ballet, opera and modern dance could serve this new concept of culture. I thought that as an aesthetic theory it was suspect, but I could see that for the purposes of the inauguration, it was pragmatic and uplifting. Afrikaans culture, which had been entombed in the Performing Arts Councils, was a sort of solid-burgher culture, a defence against radical thinking. The future of these Performing Arts Councils was under discussion. Clearly they would have to change to reflect the new society. Funding for the arts, which in the past had all been channelled through these councils in the provinces, was now the issue that was exciting arts practitioners and cultural workers. Committees with catchy acronyms were springing up everywhere in the arts as in the wider world. The argument was between those who believed that arts funding should go to the politically worthy and be controlled by a ministry of culture, or be channelled through an arts council as in Britain, independent of the government. Mongane Wally Serote, of the ANC's cultural desk, was still widely believed to favour central control, yet when I spoke to him he said he was arguing only for a full discussion of all the options. Nadine Gordimer, despite her closeness to the ANC, feared a ministry of culture and favoured an independent arts establishment.

Msomi told me that he believed that progress would be made as much by private initiative and funding as by state intervention. It struck me, as I talked to him, that the arts debate was a mirror of the national political debate. I saw, too, that following Msomi and his plans for the inauguration might be a good starting point for our film. Documentaries are fluid: emphases change, characters appear, certain scenes take on an unexpected life, and others die. In this way a documentary is far from a document but much more of a tapestry: in its early stages, before things begin to settle into place, producing a documentary can be nerve-racking because of the sense of unlimited options.

I met Nico Carstens at a café in the Market Theatre precinct. He is a tall man in his sixties, with born-again blue eyes, and the waxen skin of someone who does not go out much during the day. He was nervous, perhaps believing I was going to offer him a part in a film. The true nature of the BBC is not clear in other countries, I have discovered. We sat and drank a coffee. The Market Theatre, for all its powerful symbolism, is set in a dreary corner of Johannesburg, very different from the affluent and spotless malls where the prosperous now shop and eat. Going to the Market demands of the whites a gesture, a crossing of the tracks. Gordimer told me that the theatre had nourished the spirit during the dark years, yet in the weak winter sunshine, the whole place looked sadly neglected. There were plans to build a cultural centre across the road and an old electricity generating station would be an art gallery. The city fathers were all too aware that Johannesburg itself was becoming dangerous and run down. They feared that big business and the hotels would vacate the centre. Arts could revive neglected and devalued areas cheaply.

Nico Carstens told me that he had met Ray Phiri eighteen months before. Phiri remembered Carstens's hit, 'Zambezi', and was surprised to find that Carstens was still alive. (So was I, as a matter of fact; I hadn't heard of him since I was about fifteen.) Phiri had changed Carstens's life; he had taught him more about music in the previous few months than he could have imagined. But also – and the pale pupils gleamed – Phiri had opened his eyes socially. Carstens had been brought up in a small town in the Cape with a disregard for, rather than an antipathy towards, blacks; for many years he had never even played the same venue as blacks. Like rugby, Afrikaner music was considered offensive by blacks. Although rugby was invented in middle England, Afrikaners have appropriated it. For them rugby, as they played it, was a metaphor of their own lives; violent, physical, exclusive. I played as a student in Johannesburg; every game against an Afrikaans team was a re-run of the Boer War, particularly as the university was regarded as a hotbed of communism. (There was, literally, some truth in this. The present secretary of the Communist Party of South Africa was in my politics class.) So Carstens being clamped in a musical embrace by Ray Phiri was not just a musical fusion, but was an almost wilful act. The accordion music, *sakkie sakkie*, is the music of the small town and the closed circle. But perhaps Phiri, because of the collaboration with Paul Simon, believed in the incorporation of previously ignored musical sounds. I regret now that I did not question Carstens more closely about the exact nature of the revelations Phiri had afforded him. But it seemed that the two of them had formed a deep friendship, even love. Carstens had recorded one of the tracks on Phiri's wildly successful album, and there were plans for more. It seemed to me that this improbable friendship and collaboration might also provide some insights into the new South Africa. There is an elaborate moral ballet going on in South Africa, among blacks in relation to their participation in the struggle, and among whites in the worthiness of their motives in the new South Africa. Yet this friendship, I thought, was outside this manoeuvring.

Carstens whistled 'Zambezi' for me. What a jaunty tune! I wondered how much money it had made him back then when it had somehow transcended the narrow limit of its origins. We used to listen at school to the hit parade on Lourenço Marques Radio. In the years that had passed since 'Zambezi', Lourenço Marques had seen a revolution of Graham Greene-like futility. The revolutionary government had been replaced (and of course Albie Sachs had been injured there) and yet here I was talking to this strangely new-born Nico Carstens about a tune I had first heard on Lourenço Marques Radio. I asked Carstens if Msomi had given him the invitation to take part in the inauguration. He was stunned by the news, which I was conveying without authorisation. It would be the greatest privilege of his life to play for Nelson Mandela. He thanked me. I explained that it was nothing to do with me, but an idea of Welcome Msomi. Some weeks later I filmed Nico Carstens and Ray Phiri rehearsing together at Phiri's house in the suburbs. There was a large pool house in the barbecue area, somewhat out of proportion to the modest bungalow next to it. It is the sort of house that most white South Africans are familiar with: built in an anonymous and unselfconscious mixture of styles, with plenty of parking and fitted cupboards and wrought-iron burglar bars, as they were called in South Africa.

Phiri is rock-star lean and touched with that distinction which rock and roll conveys. The truth is that the appearance of Eric Clapton or Mick Jagger sends a shockwave through a room that no writer can expect to give off. Rock stars may be wildly overvalued on the strange Dow Jones of celebrity, but once or twice when I have been in a room with these gods, I have been all too aware that, despite myself, I am as susceptible as the next person. In South Africa, Phiri is as close to a real star as you can get. We talked and he explained how he had carried the memory of 'Zambezi' with him for many years. He asked Carstens to play 'Zambezi' on his accordion, and then they improvised African songs and *sakkie sakkie*. It turned out that, although the inauguration was now only a few weeks away, Phiri and Carstens had not yet received the call. It was quite late at night, but I rang Msomi at home and suggested that he come over. I said how moving it was and how good it would be, for the film, if he could invite them to play on camera. Msomi soon arrived with Thuli, his wife. In the very small space of Phiri's studio, with the greatest naturalness conceivable, Phiri, Welcome, Thuli and Carstens began to play and sing while we filmed. Thuli had a voice of extraordinary beauty, which I now remembered from *Poppie*. Msomi played some drums. They sang 'One Nation, Many Cultures'. This world of musicians is one from which I am excluded (Gordimer had told me that she too is unmusical, and regrets it). The unmusical are like people without children: they know they have failed to make some of the mysterious connections in life, even as they can never fully understand what they are. It seemed to me that evening that life could not offer anything more rewarding than being able to play and sing and improvise in this way. Thuli sang in Zulu and English. Phiri accompanied her on his guitar and sang too, and Carstens played his old accordion with fervour. His face, I thought, was ecstatic.

Jon, the cameraman, had achieved his own form of fusion; cramped in a kneeling position in a corner, holding the camera for an hour or so, his back seized. I left Phiri's house for a late dinner with the crew at Bellini's, in Johannesburg's northern suburbs. This is one of the strange things about South Africa; the violent shifts of location are disturbing. The white people of my parents' generation had created a small world for themselves into which Africa had to fit. But now it's the white people – 'no longer European, but not yet African' – who are increasingly required to fit into a new landscape. I had always felt an outsider in South Africa, as though only I saw the incongruities and injustices clearly – yet now I realised, as we ate some Mediterranean–Californian salad, among exquisitely made-up women and apparently successful young men, that I would never be able to see South Africa as home. It seemed that home must have a unity of purpose, so that landscape, family and belief be united in some way. The landscape of South Africa has been deeply ingrained in me but then it seemed to be disjointed and out of time, as though something has gone wrong – it manifestly has – in the synchronisation of social, political and artistic life. What price a sense of home when out there the hundreds of thousands are living in tin shacks with plastic fertiliser bags plugging the gaps? But seeing Phiri and Carstens and Welcome and Thuli together, perhaps, I thought, I had ducked out too early. But also I remembered Nadine Gordimer's strictures about the peculiar circumstances of growing up in South Africa, and the strange contortions that the personality took on. Perhaps I knew instinctively that a lifetime of immersion in South Africa would cramp and distort me.

Landscape. I have come to see that different people see the same landscape in different ways. On my wall I have a poster of Magritte's *La Condition Humaine*. Magritte said, 'This is how we see the world. We see it as being outside ourselves, even though it is only a mental representation of what we experience on the inside.' As it becomes increasingly clear that meaning is only what the brain tells us is meaning, I find myself puzzled by the contradictions in my own experiences of the world, both the interior and the exterior landscapes. But also, as I realised that evening, I have the haunting feeling that I have lacked a sense of being home.

Welcome Msomi had told me that in order to create the stages and settings for the inauguration party, he was going to have to cut down some 'bushes'. The bushes to which he was referring were the carefully planted garden terraces of the Union Buildings in Pretoria. In a huge sweep down the hill, examples of many of the indigenous flora of South Africa had been planted, to create an idealised landscape, a celebration of the indigenous plant life. And Msomi wanted to cut these bushes down. I saw then that landscapes are indeed, as Magritte said, only a recreation of what is in our minds. Why not? One man's landscape is another man's bushes. The arguments in South Africa about culture and about political dispensations often overlook these truths. It occurred to me then, eating the chargrilled tuna, that the origins of culture can be found in the myths of landscape and the associated religious thoughts, as with the Venda. If this is so, then South Africa hasn't a chance of a national identity, however optimistic the efforts of Phiri and Carstens and Msomi.

One nation, many landscapes. And around us, the prosperous but nervous white people of Johannesburg, among whom we invariably chose to eat, were discussing the meaning of the elections. Maids were going to be protected by a charter, a piece of back-door socialist nonsense. The effect would be increased unemployment. It was almost suicidal to drive a

Kombi, because they would shoot you just to steal it. And South Africa would win the up-coming World Cup, no problem.

Chapter 3

Cape Town is in my mind delimited by the shadow of the mountain. Lying just outside the shadow, in the wind which funnels off False Bay, is Langa. Like virtually every other township, in the last twenty years it has been the scene of shootings, protests and brutalisation. The brutalisation of South Africa runs very deep. I can't say whether it will remain in the bloodstream, untreatable, but I think it is true that the residents of South Africa's townships have seen too much blood flowing and known too many people killed, and probably too many killers, to get over it quickly, if indeed there is going to be a respite.

Playwright Fatima Dike has lived in Langa all her life. She loves it. This I found the most surprising thing about meeting her, her love of this dreary, sandy, dirty, windswept township. She left South Africa briefly and longed for the view from her front stoep. She wrote a poem about it which she read to me, and I realised again that landscape is all in the mind. Across the road from her home she had seen a boy have his brains blown out during a protest. She described in some detail the death of this boy and the sight of brains. She pointed out the house where the township's manager had lived, an Afrikaner, who conducted numerous liaisons with black women, and died *in flagrante*. His son used to play with Fatima and her friends, the only white boy in the place. She remembered him with a mixture of pity and amusement.

While we were talking, her children came home from parochial schools. She called them 'the coconuts', black on the outside but white inside. For some years before 1990 church schools had been free to take black children; a whole generation of coconuts is growing up. Presumably their influence will be strongly felt in the new South Africa. They talked with the accents of white South Africa. The barriers between the two worlds are, in places, coming down. Our driver told me that his children did not believe him fully when he told them that under apartheid he was not allowed to travel without a pass. My old school, Bishops, in Cape Town, has had a substantial number of black children for ten years or more. This influence is one of the most unexpected and unquantifiable aspects of the new South Africa. In one of his novels, Chinua Achebe's characters, English-educated, are still tied to the old beliefs of Africa. It may be that in the end this will achieve the fusion of which Welcome Msomi spoke, a kind of hybrid culture.

Fatima Dike had a new play starting at the Nico Malan Theatre in Cape Town. She said that the Performing Arts Councils were trying to establish their credibility by putting on her work. But so what? In her small living-room her mother sat, an elderly, genial lady with only one leg. The television was on constantly. Her children were hungry, as children always are after school, helping themselves to snacks. Outside, the rubbish appeared to have been widely spread by the wind. In the distance Table Mountain was gathering outriders of cloud. I saw then what should have been obvious, that the hopes for South Africa's future rest in a myriad of tiny actions and assertions. And also I realised that anyone who could regard this dreadful place with affection and nostalgia was a lot more rational than I.

Godfrey Moloi is known as the Godfather of Soweto. He likes this image of himself and he used the phrase on the plaque commemorating the building of his new home. Soweto is, if that is possible, an even more desolate landscape than Langa. It is attached to Johannesburg in the way that a goitre is attached to the neck. Flying over Johannesburg you can see all too clearly the design: the township separated from the town by a *cordon sanitaire* of industry, mines and highways. The axes of the roads suggest, like Haussmann's plan for Paris, some military input. From the air you can see exactly what Soweto is, a huge, barely functional refugee camp. Once I had heard Gordimer's phrase about apartheid, that it sprang from an unconscious will to genocide, it was all too easy to see the dispensation provided for black South Africans in these terms. If you long for blacks to disappear, and secretly expect it to come about one day, the arrangements are likely to be somewhat impromptu. But Soweto has entered the mythology of South Africa and the rhetoric of the struggle. This is partly because, like the Falls Road, news crews could always find a story there. But it's also because Soweto was the scene of the most bitter conflict, the schoolchildren's uprising, and it was the home of almost every prominent black person. Johannesburg and its unlovely growth was the centre of resistance.

There used to be a very small section in one of the Johannesburg newspapers called 'Window on the Townships' which provided, like aquarium plate glass, a safe and soundless view of what was going on. Most townships were invisible to white South Africans; that is how they were designed. It is still said that the vast majority of white South Africans have never visited a township. But the townships have come to occupy a special place in the mythology of the new South Africa. They are the sites of struggle, every bit as important as Nazeby or Gettysburg or Sebastopol. It is essential to the ANC to believe that it was the struggle, rather than a conversion to the merits of democracy, which brought about the change in South Africa. This myth-making is not a trivial matter: either South Africans are one nation, albeit with plenty of interesting variations, or they are a number of peoples inhabiting common boundaries reluctantly. It goes right to the heart of the political debate about a unitary versus a federal state, about minority rights against a more inclusive polity, and ultimately about the power and influence of whites.

As Simon Schama has demonstrated, landscape plays a very important part in the function of a national consciousness. What, I wondered as I entered Soweto, is the common landscape of South Africa? Is this, like Langa, the *Gemeinschaft* on which the future South Africa is to be based – what Schama has called a sentimental ethnography – and will it be nurtured in some way? Landscape. Ethnography. History. And above all, hovering like a miasma, the idea of Culture.

Godfrey Moloi owns a night-club, the Blue Fountain. Everybody's life has a defining decade, and for Moloi it was the jazz and gang decade of Orlando, in the fifties when he was squiring Miriam Makebe, playing the trumpet and the sax, and mixing with the gangs. His friends in those days were a breed of jazz musicians and gangsters who were nowadays looked on as having belonged to a golden age. Moloi's night-club is like one of those bars on the outskirts of American towns, built without too many frills. It is next door to a supermarket. Outside the night-club was an armoured police vehicle. Some British security experts, ex-Metropolitan police, were on a fraternal visit. They had been brought to the club in an armoured car. I had arrived with a driver who knew everybody, but also armed with Godfrey Moloi's advice in case of trouble: 'Say you are coming to see me.' I waited for Godfrey Moloi while he talked to the policemen. What he made of these bulky men with their jocular but slightly sinister manner and their regional accents, I couldn't guess. He sat politely among them as they drank a complimentary Lion Lager, a man in early middle age dressed in a heavy suit, his eyes which are hooded like Walter Cronkite's, watchful, in the sense that many intelligent people's are. Stupid people have dead eyes. Drunks have dead eyes.

Eventually we were introduced after the thirsty policemen had gone off in their armoured car. While we were talking, he ate. This was common to all our later meetings: he would eat breakfast or lunch while we talked. Now he was eating meat with his hands, as he waited to see what I wanted. Later he was to say something to me which I saw had some bearing on his unselfconscious eating habits: he said that he could not slaughter a sheep in the presence of the Archbishop of Canterbury. When killing a sheep as a mark of hospitality, it is essential that the guest should hear the bleat which immediately precedes its death. The sheep's agony is in earnest of the hospitality. Godfrey Moloi lives in, for him, an awkward time. He believes the culture of his people is under threat. Not to be allowed to slaughter a sheep may appear to be a small matter to those who have moved to the white suburbs, but the lack of singing at weddings and funerals is more serious. People now play tapes and CDs. In the past, in the recent past, they sang.

I asked Moloi about the future of Soweto. He looked at me warily. The politicians had already forgotten Soweto. He and Dr Motlana and Winnie Mandela, whose residence was largely symbolic, were the only three prominent people left, he said. Soweto would eventually realise that it had been forgotten and there would be a second uprising. Godfrey Moloi organised games and charity events; all the sides had tried to co-opt him in the election struggle, but he resisted. He was even-handed in his condemnations: the Zulus had been turned into non-people by calling them 'hostel dwellers'. That had only served to alienate them. There was a breakdown of respect for the older generation. The youth movement was out of control. These complaints reminded me of how Mafia bosses are reputed to speak, lamenting the passing of the codes of honour. But I soon discovered that Godfrey Moloi, although protesting that he was poorly educated, was extremely shrewd. He, of almost all the people I was to meet in South Africa, was the least inclined to subscribe to the idea of one nation. In fact he believed firmly in the maintenance of differences.

I had heard that he had built a huge new house and he offered to take me there. The streets of Soweto are frightening for the outsider, not because they loom over you, or crowd in, but because of their endlessness and anonymity. The strings of little houses are interspersed by churches, schools and besieged shopping centres. There is a feeling of alienation, as though the human qualities have been diluted. Sometimes in the deep of the land where the cold air rises in the winter, you see squatter camps, just makeshift shelters of corrugated iron, plastic and wood. If ever you needed an idea of the scale of South Africa's problems, these shacks, rising near all the cities, illustrate them with chilling clarity. In Moloi's large, but far from new, car, we progressed through these mean streets to what looked like a recently developed area. The houses, while small, are similar to the estates where white blue-collar workers lived.

We turned down a narrow road, at the end of which something akin to the Taj Mahal rose above the modest bungalows. Moloi's new home has about an acre of garden ending in a malodorous stream. The lawn has white pigeons performing quadrilles and an enormous barbecue house. The swimming pool is upstairs on a terrace. The only difference between this and a house in Sandton was the security arrangements: there are none around Moloi's home. The house is white and angular. There is an indoor stream full of Koi carp, which came puckering their large and whiskery faces to the surface when Moloi called, 'Fishies, come, fishies. Fishies, fishies,' to them. There is a bust of Moloi in one of the corridors, and a Mini Moke in the double garage. The floors and every available surface are marble. It seemed more like a mausoleum than a house. I wondered if Moloi wanted to show it to Miriam Makebe who had deserted him for the Manhattan Brothers all those years ago. Although she is back in the country, Moloi has not spoken to her.

A few weeks later, we filmed him in his house playing the saxophone very badly, and feeding his fishes. He used a striking image about the elections: they were like opening a cage of doves at midnight, he said. The doves were bemused. The young think their time has come but they have no education and no skills and very little expertise to call upon, he said.

They don't want to work but have fallen for the idea that easy money – car hijacking, drugs or burglary – is better money than money earned. Moloi in his grand house seemed to be alone, although he often organised football matches and games and charity events. He also has his coffin ready for his death at any time. We got on well, I thought, and I was flattered when he invited me to a dinner for prominent businessmen as his guest. We arrived at the appointed place in Soweto, only to be told that it had been switched to a hotel in Johannesburg. This was added confirmation that Soweto has become marginalised. As he saw it, Soweto existed only in the rhetoric of the leading politicians. I felt drawn to him because of his wilful dismissal of the party line. 'I am not against my people,' he said. 'I wouldn't live here if I was. But if the middle class leaves Soweto for white areas it means that there will be nobody to show these people the way. They are going to be like a lost flock of sheep. They are doomed.'

Moloi admits to having killed people in his youth. He said he has snake eyes which frighten his enemies. He is a strange man, but vividly intelligent, all too conscious that he is putting himself outside the mainstream, all too aware that his ideas are not going to be popular. 'I am not a man who avoids telling the truth. Our people must learn. It cannot happen overnight.'

Back in London, the South African writer Rian Malan had told me that the exciting thing about South Africa was that the categories were being confused. In the old days there were moral certainties; now there are none, villains and good people can be found on all sides. Godfrey Moloi certainly does not fit neatly into any category but it seems to me certain that the ANC and its followers have been too ready, as Godfrey Moloi told me then, to take the view that if you are not for them you are against them. He decried, too, the habit of looking backwards for blame because he sees that this is one of the biggest problems for his people, a disinclination to accept responsibility for their own lives and to build for themselves. So he thinks the trek to the white suburbs is deplorable, because it suggests an inability to do anything with Soweto.

I had curiously mixed feelings listening to Godfrey Moloi. I wanted to applaud his honesty and common sense but I also wondered if, because he had prospered in the apartheid era, he feared the end of its certainties. Someone brought up in South Africa finds it very hard to escape an exaggerated consciousness of race; once when I chased a black mugger in Stoke Newington, the overwhelming thought in my mind was that he was letting down his people, pandering to prejudice. What Godfrey Moloi was telling me was that black people in the main were not equipped, either by education or by temperament, for success in the new South Africa. He said that Soweto would become a completely lawless ghetto. To tell the truth, I thought it was already that. We agreed to meet again in a year's time. He had dressed like a sailor, for the filming. I left him looking like the skipper of a motor yacht, perhaps like the skipper in *Some Like It Hot*, in his vast marble mausoleum, thinking his own dark thoughts.

That night I played his peace video back in my hotel room. In it he begged God to spare his people.

Chapter 4

'The struggle of man against power is the struggle of memory against forgetting.' (Sometimes translated as 'the struggle of memory against oblivion'.) Milan Kundera's words are often quoted in South Africa. They are usually deployed by those who want to remember the other side's inhumanities. It seemed to me, in the days leading up to the election, that the memory of those inhumanities would be too strong, that they would bubble up in the fissures opened by the democratic process. Welcome Msomi told me that Chief Buthelezi, the leader of the Zulu Inkatha Freedom Party, was going to be buried. 'Killed?' I asked. 'Yes.' A few days later Buthelezi joined the electoral process, causing consternation to the electoral commission which had to print twenty million stickers for the ballot papers. In the middle of this I went to Durban for a literary prize-giving. As we approached in the hotel's minibus, tens of thousands of Zulus were leaving town after an election rally. I saw not the might of the Zulu nation, but massed cannon fodder, galumphing and posting and blowing whistles as they departed for their villages and townships. The Zulus have never forgotten, but it is not always clear exactly what they have not forgotten. Buthelezi is like a spurned lover, minutely examining any slight and wound. The memories, it seemed, were plenty, but the conclusions to be drawn from them were often fiercely contradictory.

The prize-giving was remarkable: prizes were awarded for

six African languages as well as for English and Afrikaans. (Modesty does not prevent me from telling you that the winner in the English section was my book, *Masai Dreaming*.) One recipient of a prize complained bitterly that the extract from his book, written in Northern Sotho, had been read by an actress who did not speak his language idiomatically. (He was angry, perhaps, because the African language prize was split three ways.) But I wondered if culture, which this prize was intended to promote, was not really about identity. Culture and identity are inseparable. Identity comes with a history. In South Africa today, I realised, the only common identity is of having suffered apartheid. Apartheid is the defining principle of South Africans in the way that the Holocaust is now the defining principle of Jews. There is, of course, one major difference: apartheid was carried out by one section of the population against another. The only possible logical way out of this dilemma is for white South Africans to claim that they, too, were victims of apartheid, that they were brutalised, duped and perverted. If, as Nadine Gordimer has said, a writer growing up in South Africa takes on strange forms, like a plant adapted to desert life, is it not plausible that whites could claim that they, too, were distorted by history? So the question of keeping memory alive is not a simple one, as I had found talking to Godfrey Moloi. And culture was not necessarily going to provide the quick fix that was demanded.

Of all the cultural organisations, the one that I had heard reviled most roundly was the Performing Arts Council of the Transvaal. This was housed at the State Theatre in Pretoria, a large, ugly, concrete building at first glance not unlike the Royal National Theatre in London. (Concrete and its affinity with the arts is a subject for a graduate thesis.) I had visited the State Theatre once, to see the opening night of *Evita* at the invitation of an actor who was playing Che Guevara. At that time, in the mid-eighties, Pretoria still gave the impression of having no inkling of what was going on beyond its stunned suburbs. These Afrikaans towns anyway have an unnatural calm, akin to the atmosphere at an embalmer's workshop. But now Pretoria had grown upwards. In my youth it was still a small, semi-rural town, and tried without much success to throw off the Calvinist dislike of public vivacity. In the eighties Breyten Breytenbach had really shocked Pretoria by accepting an award but damning with bitter words the regime which locked him up for seven years. He told me that he had refused to set foot in Pretoria, and – I think – had to be carried to the ceremony. Now one of the theatres has been named 'The Breytenbach'. I suppose I should be surprised, but I am not. Nothing is more certain than that Nelson Mandela will have his statue outside South Africa House when he dies.

George Kok was the director of the opera. We met in his office near the top of the building with wonderful views northwards, over the city and out towards the just-visible farmland. He was wearing a capacious shirt, which oscillated when he laughed. He said that the arts structures would have to be reformed. They had taken too little account of the indigenous music. He defended opera, an art form that was enjoyed by many, including the Coloured community of the Cape. But he still appeared to believe at that time that he and the board of the opera could control the pace of change and introduce picaresque African themes. I was aware that Nadine Gordimer had said the opera was still ordering wigs from Vienna for a production of *The Merry Widow*. But Kok's idea was to look for inspiration from the rural African communities. He told me that Africans still had 'camp fires' and he thought that a series of children's tales sung around the camp fire could be just the ticket. At one point he became angry and railed against 'the so-called critics' of the opera. I could see his dilemma: the subsidy of Austrian wigs, chubby tenors, rustic Italian scenery, leather jerkins and operatic fripperies is probably even harder to justify to the masses than ballet, particularly as it is not even sung in any of the eleven official languages. Kok said that they were looking forward to taking part in the inauguration. Sitwell Hartman was going to sing 'Nessun Dorma' at Welcome Msomi's invitation.

Sitwell Hartman is a stout, good-looking tenor from the Cape, with enormous power in his lungs. From a short distance away I listened to him sing 'Nessun Dorma'. When it was over, my knees were unjointed. The sound had done what an acupuncture is supposed to do: it had found all the hidden entry points to my nervous system. I felt weak and moved. Hartman confirmed that there was a tradition of opera among the people at the Cape. It had been introduced hundreds of years ago, and in his view it was as valid an art form as any in South Africa. But also, he suggested, his singing ability was a passport out, if opera ever died in South Africa. He, too, was looking forward to singing for his president.

Nearby, the ballet, under a Scottish ballet master, was rehearsing a *pas de deux* for the inauguration, and in another building the modern dance group was practising its routines. The point that the teachers made was that dance was instantly accessible to all cultures. The disciplines of ballet were of value whatever the final use the dancers might make of them. Black dancers were numerous in the modern dance group, but apparently none had so far persevered with classical ballet. And the price of tickets deterred the black audience.

So, in culture, as everywhere, the problem must be addressed. How many times I was to hear that money must be used to redress the balance in South African society. It is a seductive metaphor, this balance. There is undoubtedly an enormous gulf in wealth between white and black. Almost all the whites have been dragged up into the middle class, although now there are white beggars and tramps at many street corners; indeed, there was one sifting through the rubbish bins of the State Theatre when I arrived. But the idea of redressing the balance suggests that there are mechanisms which will achieve this: a bit more weight on this side, and the measure will even out. I fear that this is not possible. In developed Western societies the gap between the haves and the have-nots is growing: there is absolutely no prospect of a significant narrowing of the gap in South Africa in the foreseeable future, although, of course, a black administrative class and a political élite are fast emerging. But the urgent need for restoration, for the setting of the record straight, for the proper evaluation of human worth and for some understanding of the past, demand that it must be possible to redress the balance.

As in politics, so in culture: evidence of progress is required. The cultural practitioners were under strain. They were struggling to produce a coherent policy, which was strictly a policy for funding of the arts, because it was this funding which would redress the balance.

Welcome Msomi suggested that I accompany him to a meeting in Pretoria at the Union Buildings, where arrangements for the inauguration of Mandela were being made. I was eager to see the look on the faces of the officials when Msomi suggested his rearrangement of the landscape. It was to be one of the first meetings between the officials in Pretoria, exclusively white, and those who were going to inherit power in a few days' time. We were brusquely treated by the young policeman at the entrance to the Important People's car park. He wasn't impressed that Msomi was in charge of the inauguration. He was intent on searching the car and sending us to the public parking. A few days to go, and he was not yet reconciled to the prospect of taking orders from black people, I thought. We drove past the front of the building, past the president's office. Carpenters were working at erecting the stage and the amphitheatre at the top of the flight of terraces. Down below, Pretoria rose along Church Street. It rose quite high, a plausible imitation of a modern city. I remembered the low, sleepy buildings and cowed Africans. Outside Pretoria Central, the hanging jail, you could see timid groups of Africans, friends of the condemned. Breyten Breytenbach and Hugh Lewin have written movingly of their time in there. At least they came out: thousands of almost anonymous blacks were hanged.

So Pretoria seemed to me an inauspicious place for the

inauguration of Nelson Mandela. It was steeped in the old South Africa, as the policeman had demonstrated. And yet it was happening. The carpenters, one of whom was Scottish, were building not a scaffold but a stage and semicircle of seating for the dignitaries who were to come to the coronation. Away in the distance the memorial to the Voortrekkers could be seen. These Voortrekkers were brave people but also the same people who destroyed and plundered every tribe they came into contact with. When in Natal my distant ancestor, Piet Retief, was murdered by Dingaan, the Voortrekkers swore revenge. For one hundred and sixty years they had been taking that revenge. And yet here they were handing over the citadel. It was remarkable, almost surreal. Perhaps De Klerk would look out of his office, just along from the amphitheatre where the carpenters were banging and sawing, and see all this and say, 'No, I've changed my mind at the last minute.'

The inauguration committee was a large group. Among the ANC delegation I saw Aziz Pahad, now looking like a small chipper imam, a former classmate of mine at the university in Johannesburg, and someone I had glimpsed occasionally in Charlotte Street at the Natraj eating cheaply. Then I had regarded him with affectionate amusement. Now he was a man very close to Thabo Mbeki. Both had been at Sussex University. Although in South Africa at large the memory of British influence, with which I grew up, has faded, in the ANC leadership there is an intimate knowledge of British life, which I imagine has influenced many of the decisions that have been taken. The upper echelons of the ANC exiles are far more sophisticated and worldly-wise than the home-grown politicians. Thabo Mbeki, Pahad's boss, apparently played rugby at Sussex. Some whites were taking comfort from this knowledge: a man who played rugby, in their view, was well on the way to full humanity. So often over the past few years since Mandela's release I had seen this longing amongst the whites to find in blacks something familiar, something *white*. They placed some hopes in the expectation that blacks would soon see the way things were arranged in the real world. But they also imagined that they could lose power, but at the same time retain control. Very few seemed to have taken to heart Mongane Wally Serote's suggestion that they stop talking and start listening.

The committee met in full session in one of the huge panelled meeting-rooms, lavishly equipped. Many of them were members of the interim government but with the ANC in the ascendant and clearly in charge, my old chum Aziz Pahad to the fore. They soon sped off in their cars, leaving those directly involved with the inauguration behind. I followed Msomi to another meeting in another carpeted and panelled room. On one branch of the table, which was very long and shaped like a wishbone, sat the technicians and civil servants, on the other, the representatives of the arts who were preparing for the entertainment.

It wasn't planned this way, but the contrast between the brown-suited, nervous, occasionally truculent white men on one side of the table, and the animated polyglot representatives of the arts community on the other, was stark. Msomi sat at the head of the table; among the representatives of the arts was his wife, Thuli, in a coterie of women which I was beginning to recognise from ballet and modern dance and other groups. Msomi explained the nature of the event, to the bemusement of the officials and the technical people to his left. Some of them took a plain man's view: all they wanted was a timetable and the exact locations of the various stages among the soon-to-be-uprooted bushes. Others wore a look of eager interest, as if this seminar on the new realities was of vital importance to them. On the other side of the table, the arts workers giggled and gossiped. An old jazz man from the romantic Sophiatown era, Johannesburg's golden age, amused the women on his left effortlessly. I longed to know what he was saying to them.

Msomi soon ran into trouble. Richard Cock said that on his rough time estimates the show was going to run two or three hours over length. Msomi seemed a little impatient with this carping. He was painting in broad brushstrokes. He explained how the huge choir would file in. Cock and others asked if the choir could be expected to spend eight or nine hours without food or a lavatory break. Msomi turned to the nuts and bolts men. They would try to sort something out, he said. And so it went on. Occasionally ANC ideologues would deliver a small pep talk on the significance of the occasion. But it was not lost on anybody, not least the white men in the cheap suits, the way things were going when Msomi outlined plans for a hundred *sangomas* – witch-doctors – to take part.

In a break, I talked to Mongane Wally Serote. He denied that he was for a ministry of culture which would decide every aspect of arts funding. In fact all he wanted was a full discussion of every aspect of the arts. He had the look of a refugee, I thought, a tired face, eyes suggesting that nothing would surprise him. In his recent poetry he has proclaimed the universality of the human spirit. What he said at the Union Buildings that day as the South African flag fluttered in its death throes and the carpenters built the stage for the new president didn't sound as doctrinaire as I had been led to believe: he said that there was no future unless black and white co-operated. I saw no obvious signs of excitement, only weariness, yet in his collection of poetry, *Third World Express*, he had been anticipating this day:

One morning, my people will hang on a sunrise.
We shall stand face to face with the sun . . .
we shall have buried apartheid – how shall we shake hands? . . .
How shall we hug each other?
What first words will we utter?

I gazed across the valley to the Voortrekker Memorial, placed on a hill across the valley, directly in the sight line of Herbert Baker's building. As you get older you begin to see, sometimes with unwanted clarity. Here you hardly needed any imagination to see the impermanence of certainty.

Chapter 5

I realised as I drove back to Johannesburg that, much as I wanted to, I couldn't subscribe to the notion that culture would provide anything more than a temporary rallying point for the new nation. In the end, I thought, the ethnic identities would prevail over the supranational identity. Even to think this was painful, because apartheid was built on the premise that people of different races and cultures could never live together in harmony. But there is a difference: apartheid proclaimed that white culture and white identity were more real, more tangible and more significant. It's not really the century in which to proclaim the superiority of western behaviour, even if it is true that western culture and science have prevailed. What worried me then, and worries me now, is that ethnic identity, always allied to culture, is a more basic unit of political currency than an idealised nationhood. The reluctant Inkatha Zulus were taking part in the elections, but only because, for the moment, they thought that was the best way of protecting themselves.

Msomi's slogan, 'One nation, many cultures', was, in effect, the ANC's election campaign set to music. Nadine Gordimer in the last fifteen years or so has identified herself with the ANC because she believes that the ANC is more than a political party. Although she recognises the pitfalls of a writer's proclaiming an interest, and believes she has kept her writing rigorously apart, she nonetheless believes that her own journey is towards home: 'I had no lineal connection with the past around me . . . I had the most tenuous of connections with the present.' Her life and work have been a process of trying to close the existential gap that whites experience, of being no longer European, but not yet African. Without wishing to condense or minimise her life's work, it seems to me that her seminal act of reconciliation was to identify with the liberation movement as fully as was possible for a successful writer living in relative safety and prosperity. She has called this process 'the transformation of my place'. She began to make her writing part of what Barthes has called 'the essential gesture of the writer'; she 'entered the communality of my country'. But Gordimer, like all of us white South Africans, could say 'my country' but not 'my people'. Gordimer believed, and I don't dispute it for a moment, that she and other whites had come into their own at last. In Serote's phrase, they were now able to utter their first words to other people.

During my childhood the Pretoria Road was a country road peopled by Ndebele bead-sellers emerging from their colourful huts at the sight of a car. Now it is a busy highway, and Pretoria and Johannesburg are only separated by a few miles of grassland which is being nibbled from all sides. The towers of Johannesburg were visible in the last rays of the sun, like the religious paintings of Jerusalem in Jackson Hlungwane's scrapbooks. I was thinking, in relation to myself, what South Africa as a home means. Gordimer's idea that Africans had the certainty that they were coming home one day touched me. I have lived in England since I was twenty, longer than I have lived in South Africa, yet I have always felt the pull of the landscape and the people of South Africa. Living in London is for me a continuing pleasure, and I have written novels about London and Londoners twice now with affection and some intimacy, but I have always felt this sense that home was elsewhere, although not necessarily in South Africa. I was also all too aware that my own, bitter-sweet, alienation was not a matter of great significance: after all, I had chosen to leave as soon as I decently could, and the reasons were not simply and nakedly 'political'. Let me digress for a moment: it always seemed to me that there were no politics in South Africa until the eighties. The issue was one of human rights rather than politics. Democratic politics 'welcomes perpetual non-violent controversy', to quote from a handbook on democracy I happen to have on my desk as I write. What has happened in South Africa is that the era of human rights abuse, abuse on an almost inconceivable scale, has ended and an era of politics has begun. My own decision to leave was because of a reluctance to live in the contorted way forced on white South Africans. 'The old is dying and the new cannot be born; in this interregnum there arrives a great diversity of morbid symptoms,' as Antonio Gramsci wrote, and which Gordimer used as an epigraph for *July's People*. To my mind, as I drove along the highway with that intensity of feeling you get under big skies thinking expansive thoughts, the fact that the interregnum was declared over did not necessarily mean that the white man's dilemma was in any way resolved. It struck me that perhaps Gordimer had so identified the moment of freedom and had been so intensely devoted to the idea of her own, and her country's, transfiguration, that she may have underestimated the problems of the new South Africa. I was not thinking here of servant shortages and car hijackings or higher taxes, but of exactly the kind of existential problem of identity she had been grappling with in her work for forty years. For example, if it is clear that the Zulu people wish to break away from the unitary state because they fear for their identity, and if it is true that a number of whites would rather live servantless and isolated in remote parts of the country than join the party, what price this new liberated persona? And what sort of home will it be, if the unitary state has to be preserved for the foreseeable future by the army? And what if it was true, and increasingly visible, not only that the hand-over of power was in fact 'deal-driven' as Van Zyl Slabbert had said, but also as a signal for the emergence of new oligarchies, and that the culture which Msomi was promoting was in reality simply an opiate to disguise the electoral truth? And, what was more important, if the violence in the townships and the rural areas continued to bleed on to the marriage bed of national unity? Violence in South Africa is like a psychotic relative locked in the attic, rumbling, moaning, audible but still just about chained to the bedpost. If violence overwhelms South Africa, where would this transfiguration be?

Culture is also tied to history, real or imagined places, invented or remembered events. Take Blake and Albion, or Wagner and the Teutonic gods, or Thoreau and Walden Pond. The Afrikaner and the Covenant, the Zulu and Isandhlwana, the Indians and Gandhi. There is no end to the competing myths and antipathetic symbols. How could a culture be united to cover all these? And, as I had found in Venda, there are some powerful mythologies hardly known in the wider world by which people lived their lives. The frailty of rational thought is one of the most salutary lessons of our century, and yet here in South Africa a euphoric sense of transfiguration had seized many rational people.

I passed a spot on the road where, as a boy, I had taken my pony and, with some friends, spent the night camped by a stream. We had tethered our ponies and tried to sleep on the hard, tick-infested ground. All these rivers and streams and rolling hills had been grazed and farmed by the Ndebele until the Natives Land Act of 1913 had begun the process of removing the Africans from their own land. When we camped near here, there were still a few huts and a trading store, but even then it was clear which way things were going. Now a factory stood where the store had been and the Ndebele, like the Wampanoag Indians of Martha's Vineyard, had vanished into the fissures of the new order.

When I was at school in South Africa, nobody taught us about the Natives Land Act of 1913, a piece of legislation which dispossessed hundreds of thousands of Africans and created a landless, impoverished and therefore subjugated people. I first heard of it when reading about Sol Plaatje –

author, translator, journalist, polemicist and first secretary of the ANC – only a few years ago. (I am ashamed to say I hardly knew of Sol Plaatje until then.) The physical effects of this process were all too clear – rural slums for the blacks and endless rolling spaces for the whites. But when I thought of my ignorance as a boy, I wondered what the effect of the disinterment of South Africa's history would be, and whether the culture of South Africa was so malleable that it could possibly encompass the shocks of history to come. Far from coming into the light, perhaps South Africans were really only in a chiaroscuro, a moral state as dangerous but far more ambiguous than the one they had left behind.

The Sisulus and the Mandelas are tied together: Mandela's first wife was a relative of the Sisulus. Albertina Sisulu has represented for many the true face of African womanhood throughout Walter Sisulu's, Mandela's close associate's, long imprisonment. Her dignity and charm are legendary. There is a sinister link between the families which is disturbing: the killing of Abubaker Asvat, Winnie Mandela's doctor. Albertina Sisulu was Asvat's nurse and receptionist. Two youths visited the surgery and gave false details of their names on the in-patient card which she filled in. These youths killed Dr Asvat as Albertina was working in the dispensary. The manager of Winnie Mandela's football team, Mandela United, Jerry Richardson, had been to the surgery the night before. It was Winnie herself who suggested that the murder might in some way be tied to the investigations into the killing of Stompie Moeketsi Seipei. The theory that Asvat was about to give evidence under subpoena about his examination of Stompie shortly before he died, and had to be killed, was never fully investigated, but it is known that there were links between the killers and Jerry Richardson.

Zwelakhe Sisulu is one of the sons of Albertina and Walter Sisulu. At the time of the election he was chief assistant to the CEO of the SABC, but it was known that he would be taking over sooner rather than later. It seemed to me that

Sisulu and the SABC would play a big role in any future debate about culture, perhaps a bigger role than all the competing arts organisations. I was thinking of Britain in my lifetime and the role the BBC and the other companies have played in creating a national self-image. In Britain it was not done by vivid displays of nationalism, but by an insider's sense of what was appropriate. The establishment was able to accommodate the strangely turbulent creativity of British society at large. However the process worked, it was clear to me that television had defined the British for the last thirty years. If I was right in fearing that ethnicity might become the basic unit of political currency, I wondered how the SABC was going to regard that, and how far the SABC would feel itself obliged to follow the ANC line, which after all was a political one, in matters of culture.

Sisulu is quite a solid-looking man with narrow, almost oriental eyes. He has been detained and he has worked in journalism and been a Nieman Fellow at Harvard. Compared with senior white executives I had met at the SABC, Sisulu is a mandarin of charm and sophistication. He saw immediately the thrust of my questions: first, he said, people like him who had been involved in the struggle would be able both to stand up to the new government if required to do so, and second they were all too aware that lapses in standards of probity and impartiality were going to be judged even more harshly because of who they were. As regards the culture, he was in the process of preparing proposals for the future of broadcasting to the Independent Broadcasting Authority. It sounded good, but the SABC were largely active ANC supporters. For example, one of its new governors, Fatima Meer, had rushed out a statement supporting Winnie Mandela in 1991. Nonetheless, Sisulu understood the need for complete independence of the SABC: the democracy he had in mind was not of the one-party variety even though at that time, in 1994, it was not certain that all members of the ANC could see much point in independent institutions. But Sisulu also saw the problems of culture which the interim constitution had enshrined by ordaining eleven official languages; in practice, however, English was going to be the lingua franca.

It was a brief meeting, but I had the strong impression that Zwelakhe Sisulu had inherited his famous father's talents. I wondered, though, whether someone who had experienced what he and his family had would not always be bound to the movement. It would be understandable. But there was also the question of the Mandela connection: what had his mother, Albertina, to say about the murder of Asvat? She had helped to rescue boys who had become ensnared in Winnie's football team, which seems to have been a very sinister cover for torture and beatings rather than anything to do with soccer. And what did Walter, his father, think about the ascendancy of Nelson Mandela? Many people in South Africa have forgotten that in the sixties Robert Sobukwe, of the PAC, was a bigger name than Mandela, and that the ANC's fortunes fell very low at some points in the seventies, only really reviving with the UDF's campaign in the eighties. In her husband's absence in prison, Albertina had become Transvaal president of the UDF while Winnie was in exile in Brandfort. Winnie had come to regard herself as the sovereign power and she was suspicious of the ANC and of Albertina. The Sisulus are no lightweights and perhaps they, rather than the Mandelas, are the first family of South Africa. Nobody could imagine a member of the Sisulu family recommending necklacing as a means of advancing the political struggle. And nobody in South Africa needed reminding that it was Winnie Mandela who did so in April 1986. There are key moments in history when opinion turns and perceptions change. Winnie's enthusiastic advocacy of necklacing led to a widespread reappraisal of the mother of the nation.

But I found no easy way of assessing the ANC leadership. Perhaps what Breyten Breytenbach told me is true: they have a core of ruthlessness forged in the struggle; perhaps their experience is just too remote from those of us who have not been willing to join in. I could see that Nadine Gordimer was looking for a communion with the struggle and its activities which was – in the end – unobtainable. (A homosexual friend once told me that the paradox of homosexuality is that homosexuals are always looking for real men, but that by definition real men are unobtainable.) The leadership of the ANC have this remoteness: they have seen and they have experienced things which will never be experienced by us or be visible to us. Also, it was possible, I thought, that the ANC had calculated that only by embracing democratic institutions wholeheartedly and by ignoring the statist aspects of their charter would they be able to succeed in the modern world. I wondered if, given the choice, they wouldn't have preferred the command economy and the benign one-party state. I wondered if pragmatism had not prevailed over principle.

Shortly after the election, Zwelakhe Sisulu took over as head of the SABC. His brother Max became chairman of the Parliamentary Select Committee on Reconstruction and Development. Reconstruction and Development soon became the mantra of South Africa, the secular answer to all present ills. The Sisulus were there at the heart of things as usual.

I was grappling with this notion of culture; it had occurred to me that South Africans are now defined by apartheid. Primo Levi says that he and the other Italian Jews were hardly aware of being Jewish until they were deported. Now of course the defining principle of Jewishness is the Holocaust. And now all South Africans, white or black, are called upon to make their accommodation with apartheid. Many whites have found that they were deceived and their lives cruelly stunted by the pseudo-science of apartheid. To some, like Van Zyl Slabbert, the revelation came early, in his case while he was a student at Stellenbosch; to others it has come very late, but they, too, can claim to be victims. In obvious ways they were prevented from taking their full part in the world. Spiritually they were oppressed and misled by the belief in apartheid. For blacks in general and for the activists in particular, apartheid has been the dominant factor in their lives. Apartheid has been both a physical and a mental barrier. It has closed to them many areas: it has removed a whole black generation from education and it has butchered and degraded tens of thousands.

But I had a maverick thought: apartheid, strangely, is also a blessing. Black South Africans have an immense amount of spiritual capital in the bank and God knows they have earned it. It has given them, just as it has given Nelson Mandela, a status above all other people in the world at the present time. Whites, although many of them have been involved in many ways in the struggle, are ultimately denied this acknowledgement, with the possible exception of the Umkhonto activists. But even they are seen, I believe, as outsiders who dedicated themselves to the cause of others for particular ideological reasons.

What this meant was that apartheid is the only unifying factor in the country. Apartheid will become the myth, around which everybody can gather in his or her own way. Apartheid will be the touchstone of all decisions. Apartheid will in effect be the culture of South Africa, the defining principle of the new society. Everyone can join in. From Nadine Gordimer to the most bestial prison warder, on the white side; from Nelson Mandela to the Venda maidens dancing naked by firelight on the black side; nobody in South Africa is untouched by apartheid. Nobody in South Africa can avoid assessing themselves in relation to it. The one nation with many cultures I realised referred to the children of apartheid. The *Sozialen Gedächtnisses* of South Africa will be of apartheid: that is all they have to fall back on. The essential cultural myth of the new South Africa is this: something significant will rise from the pyre of apartheid.

Chapter 6

As always in Johannesburg, I found myself exhilarated and deeply disturbed by turns. It is a jumpy city with hostility and lawlessness breathing ever more closely on the neck of the white suburbanites. But the air itself, rather short of oxygen, is invigorating and the evenings are almost invariably uplifting. African twilight comes and goes quickly, but it induces a feeling of optimism and grandeur. Some whites told me that the new tension in the air was an added stimulant, something like that which war correspondents feel. Whenever I am in Johannesburg I find myself moving fast and purposefully, as if I am responding to some rhythm.

It's an ugly place. And the city now resembles an encampment, with virtually every building either heavily guarded or encircled with barbed wire. But I was able to find places where I had drunk, as a boy of eighteen and nineteen, prodigious amounts of beer and brandy and cheap white wine. There was one bar down near the City Hall which was unchanged, except that early in the night the clientele was thinning out fast. Apparently the Rhodes Scholars who make up the board of Anglo American now hardly see the town: they enter an underground car park, work all day, feed within 44 Main Street, and exit as fast as possible. Africa has come to Johannesburg in a big way, where once visitors found it surprisingly un-African.

I used to go home from rugby practice at the university to

our little house in Barkly Road, just below Nadine Gordimer's. And now I saw the students practising rugby there, just as I had, and I remembered physical details like the dryness of the kikuyu grass (grass so dry that it burned the skin if you were tackled), and the rasping thinness of the air in the lungs. And I remembered our coach, Syd Newman, telling us that he was the only person in the history of rugby who could put in a perfect cross-kick while running straight ahead: for the rest of us he recommended a slight turn infield. And I remembered going out into the veld completely drunk with my fellow editors of *The Disenchanted*, one of whom is now a professor at Warwick University, to destroy an electricity pylon. We had no dynamite, but I think we imagined in our brandy-inflamed state that such details were bourgeois. One of my fellow editors was later arrested and held briefly. He warned us that he had cracked in five minutes and given them our names. We didn't care.

And as always when I return to Johannesburg I was astounded by the changes. It is a ruthless place. Huge buildings and offices and business parks and innumerable restaurants have covered square miles of veld where we used to ride and chase guinea-fowl and commune with nature. We were surprisingly ignorant of nature: we tried to shoot it with our pellet guns. Now the northern suburbs have become ecological: every other person is off bird-watching or whale-spotting or rhino-tracking. In nature and its preservation the white people have found a new way to impose themselves. Eco-imperialism has arrived.

For all this, Johannesburg has a magic for me. I have been to and lived in far more beautiful places, places with many more attractions. In fact I have rarely visited any less appealing places. But I suppose landscape works its way under your skin when you are young and lodges there for ever. This makeshift place, a place which, like Los Angeles, has comfort for the well-to-do without dignity for the poor, and grandeur and nobility for no one, is in many ways still totally familiar. The scent of gardens; the clamour of frogs; the impatience of the insect life; the bleached afternoons; the melting evenings. And other things far more basic, like the little cafés selling meat pies and crisps ('chips', in South African pronounced 'sheeps' by the blacks, and 'cherps' by the whites). What's the point of these memories and the associations they stir? Almost everyone I know who was brought up in Africa feels this affinity to the landscape, as if the hills and the plains and even the suburban gardens are more real and more seductive and more significant than those in Europe or America where they find themselves. When I walked with the Masai in Tanzania a few years ago, I saw that their notion of the landscape was prescribed by cattle. Distant hills are described in metaphorical relation to the colours of cattle, and other places are valued because they produce green grass for cattle. And now I had seen that Welcome Msomi regarded the landscape of the Union Building as 'bushes'. Indeed it is true that landscape, as Thoreau says (and Simon Schama concurs), is entirely a self-generated notion.

These were the thoughts that troubled me as I contemplated the future of South Africa, which I was trying to understand through its culture. Isaiah Berlin says that the most powerful blow ever dealt to Western culture was the realisation that cultures are relative and that they spring from circumstances peculiar to that society. This realisation has come late to South Africa, but I was wondering in that strange fraught week of South Africa's first election, not so much about the electoral numbers and the participation of the Zulus, as about the very basic springs of belief in South Africa, upon which this culture could be based. Sometimes I wondered if I was the only person thinking along those lines. For South Africa seemed to be taking refuge in cliché. Clichés, as is well known, provide an uncomplicated simulacrum of certainty, but the eruption of cliché in South Africa had reached a near-seismic proportion, and the single greatest cliché, repeated *ad nauseam*, was this: *We must work together*. The more Hobbesian view, that the people had been flung together and would have to minimise the conflicts, was not often expressed because, of course, apartheid was dead and apartheid stood for the differences among people.

At the Windybrow Theatre, a large Edwardian house on the very edge of the city of Johannesburg, I went to watch a rehearsal of *Julius Caesar* by a non-racial cast. The director was John Matshikiza, the son of the man who brought *King Kong* to the outside world, the musician Todd Matshikiza. John had been brought up in Lusaka and London and had worked in London as an actor and director before going home to a home he had never seen. The artistic director of the theatre was Walter Chakela, once a community theatre director who had been appointed by the Performing Arts Council of the Transvaal, presumably in order to deflect criticism of tardiness in responding to the demands of the new South Africa. But he was a shrewd man who was making the most of his opportunity. *Julius Caesar* was a set work for the Matric exams, so guaranteeing an audience.

The rehearsal was extraordinarily powerful although some of the actors were barely comprehensible. Caesar was played by a large Afrikaner with a wonderful voice. His limbs were large and loose, like a once-useful number eight. (Almost all Afrikaners have played rugby in their youth, and it shows in battered faces and stiff knees.) The director took the actors through the assassination at the Capitol. The conspirators came toyi-toying to do their work. Caesar's words, 'I am constant as the northern star,/ Of whose true-fix'd and resting quality/ There is no fellow in the firmament' seemed doubly poignant in the shifting, uncertain world that the production portrayed. Like modern dress productions of Shakespeare, there is a quick return on this kind of production which gives contemporary significance to the events on stage. But I wondered as I watched the polyglot cast – Calpurnia was black, a returnee from drama school in Cardiff – what the underlying message was. That Shakespeare, by being universal, was applicable to all societies, essentially the Harold Bloom view? Or that in South Africa a new, perhaps contrived, relevance is required of the arts? Sitting there in the dark, watching this rehearsal on the edge of the restless, edgy city, was itself a disconcerting experience because the production suggested all too clearly that assassination and violence were not abstracts in this town.

The problems of value; how does South Africa now apportion value?

That night I went to talk to Dolly Rathebe, one of the legendary jazz singers from the Sophiatown era of the fifties. So lost in legend is she, that nobody had turned up to hear her sing in a steak 'n' hamburger restaurant in the northern suburbs. A group of salesmen, sitting as far away from the band as they could, ignored her: they had come for the steaks. She is said to have an even better voice than Miriam Makeba, and she certainly belted out all sorts of numbers like 'Sweet Georgia Brown'. I have never been able to respond to jazz but now I found myself, the only fan, tapping my feet and moving my head like a nervous ostrich, trying to suggest I was lapping it all up. She and I talked in the interval. She has had a hard life, and has the sense that she missed some turnings early on, turnings which Miriam Makeba took. Makeba, I saw, had towered over the shanties and townships of Johannesburg: in her success in America those who were left behind saw a miracle, a transfiguration. But for Dolly nothing like this had happened. She had lived through the worst of apartheid, when every car journey at night was an invitation to arrest, and every precarious engagement was a triumph over the laws restricting movement, and the sheer difficulties of life for blacks. (Miriam Makeba has been involved in six serious car accidents, a hair-raising insight into the life of Africa and African musicians.) Yet here was Dolly, with the new era beckoning, singing to nobody in a hamburger joint, her struggles and travails unrecognised by the group of salesmen eating their hamburgers. They had rat-tails of hair hanging over their collars, and moustaches. I realised suddenly who it was that so many white men in South Africa reminded me of: Bruce Grobbelaar, the former

Liverpool goalkeeper. It had been puzzling me for days. Dolly, too, had received the summons from Msomi to take part in the inauguration: she was pleased, but I thought that perhaps the new era was puzzling to her. Nelson Mandela has said that being released from jail took some adjustment after the certainties that ruled there. Perhaps there are people in South Africa who will be unable to leave the confines of apartheid without being blinded.

The roads in the sprawling northern suburbs are not well lit. Remembering the warnings against stopping or being followed or being held up at road blocks, I drove fast. These were the streets where as teenagers we had partied frantically and sometimes fatally. Ivan Vladkin, the son of an elderly white Russian military man, had been killed in a car crash on this very road.

Noam Chomsky used to talk of a universal grammar, which reveals the essential properties of mind. Language is obviously a product of evolution in that modes of thinking have not developed independently of the world and society. And so, equally certainly, language is not a benison given to the human race as an amusement or a relief from the daily grind of hunting and gathering. But I wondered, as I drove along the broad, empty streets, past the endless acre plots containing comfortable Californian-style houses, whether the language of South Africa was up to the challenge of the new South Africa. It seemed to me limping along behind the band, unable to catch up. A dreadful barrenness of language was everywhere apparent. I am well aware that the demeaning of language is commonplace, and also that this is nothing whatever to do with the universal grammar, but I wondered if the debasement of language did not in some way reflect the debasement of human qualities in South Africa. And, because language was impoverished, perhaps it restricted thinking about the future of South Africa. (Driving down deserted roads late at night encourages these expansive thoughts.) It was certainly true that the language of apartheid and the language of the struggle were both desperately threadbare. When Winnie Mandela issued her endorsement of necklacing (the extraordinarily barbaric practice of putting a rubber tyre around someone's neck, filling it with petrol and then igniting it), no doubt she thought that she was speaking from within some historical tradition. 'Necklacing' was probably as attractive a word to her as 'liquidate' to the Stalinists. She regarded words as tools, or, in a phrase I heard many times, as weapons of the struggle.

Stephen Watson, South Africa's foremost essayist, gives an example of the standard of discussion in a local literary magazine: 'It should be pointed out that the relationship between literature in general and politics or history is not conceived in terms of a determinist sub-ordination of the former, but in terms of a complexly mediated dialectic, whereby neither history nor literature is prioritised.' It is too much like shooting fish in a barrel to parody this, but Watson says it is a typical contribution. His conclusion is that 'the cultural desert has penetrated the inner being, establishing nullity as its archetype'.

I discussed this proposition with Andries Oliphant, one of South Africa's leading arts activists and a recognised poet and essayist himself. He was, at that stage, fighting for the establishment of an entirely independent arts council funded from central government but not controlled in any way by a Ministry of Culture. He was critical of Watson's view. Watson, he felt, had failed to move with the times. He was hankering for the old Eurocentric certainties. But, I pointed out, in another of his essays Watson, a university lecturer, describes his own inability to be certain of anything in the gathering frenzy of the eighties. Oliphant was not impressed. He too believed in the flowering of culture which would bloom on the ashes of the old South Africa. I knew one of Oliphant's poems, a moving account of being translocated from the place where he had lived with his family as a child to a bare patch of veld. I could see that a man who has this deep scar of apartheid in his flesh might be intolerant of a university lecturer who was trying to find himself in the moral quagmire of South Africa. But I was still surprised by the bitterness of Oliphant's attack on Watson. It seemed to me to indicate how deep the philosophical divisions in South African society ran. It also demonstrated the pervasiveness of what Harold Bloom has called the 'Franco-Heideggerian psycholinguistics of Jacques Lacan and company'. Oliphant suggested to me that Watson had not studied history or deconstructed the literature sufficiently. The message was clear. Right-thinking people had a way out of the mess. Oliphant was locked in a deadly struggle with the ideologues at the time, and he was unequivocally on the side of independence and against any form of authoritarianism. For all that, it seemed that some progressive views were more progressive than others. I find myself, at the risk of being castigated as unprogressive, with Bloom; the unconscious is not a system of phonemes but a metaphor, nor is literature an unconscious history written by interested parties.

Johannesburg. Out in his palace in Soweto, Godfrey Moloi was thinking his dark thoughts. Up in Parktown, Nadine Gordimer was seeing her life's work fall into place, in Yeovil Andries Oliphant was churning out discussion papers, in his pastel office Welcome Msomi was planning the great inauguration spectacle, over in Kempton Park Ray Phiri and Nico Carstens were dreaming of a musical fusion; at Dorkay House on the edges of the city the old jazz singers were giving their all; and at the Windybrow Theatre, Romans were falling on their swords and each other's. Further out, in Pretoria, Sitwell Hartman was conserving his voice with honey and lemon, and a small ballerina was hurling herself into the air in preparation for her duet.

South Africa was ready. The time was now.

PART II

1995

Chapter 7

> In this way serious sport has nothing to do with fair play. It is bound up with hatred, jealousy, boastfulness, disregard of all rules and sadistic pleasure and witnessing violence; in other words it is war minus the shooting.
>
> *George Orwell*

I have often wondered what sport signifies. My conclusion is that sport is a simulacrum of perfection: every game, every contest, is a ritual of the desire for perfection. Charles Lamb said, 'Man is a gaming animal. He must always be trying to get the better in something or other.' This, like so much else, is Darwinian. And now I realise for the first time that this chimes with what Isaiah Berlin says about Western culture, namely that it rests on a belief in the possibility of perfection. Sport, like dreaming, seems to provide an alternative and, in some ways, more perfect, way of living life for many people, mostly men. In sport they see conflict and immediate resolution and a finite entity. Sports, even cricket, don't last long. Yet politics and political conflict are interminable and very often they don't produce a result. But sport is wonderfully simple. And it only engages one part of the mind.

1995 was Rugby World Cup year for South Africa. South Africa was staging the event for the first time as a reward for good behaviour. Rugby was white South Africa's favourite sport, not only because South Africans are generally bigger than the opposition and have a taste for violence, but because in their increasingly restricted universe, rugby at least was unambiguous. In the outside world there were only uncertainties, and at home there was downright hostility. White South Africans, for all their protestations about the beneficence of apartheid, have known from the beginning that there was something selfish, to put it at its best, about it. And they have known that blacks hated apartheid and them for putting it in place. Only rugby provided them with a haven away from the world of what they called politics, except of course that eventually politics unravelled rugby. Shrewd people saw that by curtailing opportunities to play rugby, they were undermining white South Africa's dream life and destroying its bulwark against the realities around them.

So, hosting the World Cup was perhaps an unjustified reward for white South Africa, although as it turned out the rugby cemented the loyalty of white South Africans to Mandela. Mandela hijacked the World Cup: 'Our boys, our children, our stars.' He called the Boks, the *Amabokke*. He put them in touch with the more sympathetic side of their own personalities. He introduced them to *ubuntu*, common humanity.

In truth, for South Africans rugby was pure Clausewitz, war by other means. The most famous tackle in the history of South African rugby was Mannetjies Roux's tackle on England's elegant Richard Sharp in 1962. This tackle did much in the eyes of Afrikaners to ease the pain of defeat in the Boer War. The injury to Sharp, which put him out of the tour, was regarded as an entirely appropriate payback. At that time I was playing rugby for the university Under-19 team in Johannesburg; the levels of hatred and violence were, as I have said, frightening. These people, like the Weimar Germans, had a grievance.

Mandela knew that by appropriating the World Cup he could achieve more to win over the whites in a few weeks than by years of debate. He could demonstrate to them in this way that he understood them. It seemed not to matter to them that there was so little to understand, namely that the opportunity to play and support rugby freely was more important to many than a political voice. But also I think there was something mischievous in the way he took over the spectacle and even wore the green and gold. I am sure in the cabals of the ANC there was many a chuckle. Mandela seems to have had an almost anthropological interest in the Afrikaner and what makes him tick. In 1990, when he was in jail in Paarl, Winnie was horrified on a visit to see him that he demonstrated his newly-found skills of the barbecue, the *braai*, which was a symbol of Afrikanerdom.

When I returned to South Africa in April of 1995, things were in a curious state after a year of the new government. Deputy President Thabo Mbeki's car had been stolen twice. Members of the Red Army Band had been mugged three times. The coming World Cup dominated the newspapers; Chester Williams, the Springbok wing, and his injuries were discussed at length in the prints. An argument was raging about the purchase of new Corvettes for the navy and Winnie Mandela, now the Deputy Minister of Culture, was trying to ignore the visit of Queen Elizabeth. But also there was a general astonishment: everything had changed but nothing had changed.

My plan was to finish the filming for the BBC and then to follow the progress of the World Cup. But first I went to see Godfrey Moloi in Soweto. His club, the Blue Fountain, was gloomy, as night-clubs are out of hours. There have been some wonderful movies made in night-clubs, because behind the glamour there is always a hard and implacable man whose interests extend some distance. As before, Godfrey tucked into a large meal as we were talking. He appeared to have forgotten me entirely. He had even forgotten the filming of less than a year before, when we had encouraged him to play his saxophone and feed his whiskery fishes for the camera. If the club was gloomy with its little gerry-built fountain,

Godfrey Moloi was even gloomier. He was wearing heavy tweeds, so that with his small moustache he looked like a retired general in the Indian Army. He warmed to my questions, however. The prominent people of Soweto had been reduced in number since our last conversation. Nthatho Motlana, physician and businessman, had gone, even though he had made a promise to stay. Soweto was ripe for recolonisation. He had been hearing about the case after Rwanda for the recolonisation of Africa. Soweto was now in the same condition. The whites with the economic power and muscle were coming. The successful blacks should have stayed. I found myself wondering how scientific his analysis was. But he went on to say that crime was even worse than it had been a year before. The young, he said, thought that it was their time. They must come into their own by whatever means were available, and crime was the only one. Apartheid was now the excuse for everything. Moloi gave me a quick rundown on the history of political change since 1984. The ANC, in his reckoning, beat off all challengers, first from the PAC, then from AZAPO and Black Consciousness and finally, since 1988, from the Inkatha Freedom Party. The ANC had been involved in every phase of violence. He told me that if he understood what federalism means, he was for it. There was no such thing as one nation. Everybody in South Africa looked different and had a different culture. He said that a federalist is not being selfish: he didn't want the whole country, only his corner. He told me that he wanted to preserve his own culture. And then he repeated the analogy which I remembered so vividly from our first talk: he said that if he had visitors he must demonstrate his hospitality by killing a sheep, which he could not do for the Archbishop of Canterbury. (I wondered if this was true. The Anglican Church is so multiculturally sensitive that you could probably throw a maiden to crocodiles in front of the Synod without too much tut-tutting.)

His culture, in which he felt easy, was not acceptable in the new world of the suburbs. Why, he asked, didn't they build a Sandton here in Soweto rather than running off to join the whites? He went further: those blacks wanted their children to go to white schools, and the fewer blacks there were at those schools the better they liked it. In the course of our long discussion I saw that what he was alarmed about was the abrogation of responsibility for their own destiny by blacks. Constantly he came back to the view that blacks must advance themselves in business and in education; they could not simply hitch up to the white wagon. If they did so, they would be unable to attend to their own culture. The bleating of sheep and the singing at weddings and the extended demands of family would become memories.

In the late seventies I made a film about King Sobhuza of Swaziland. Sobhuza was a remarkable man, much loved by black and white. His dilemma was, I thought, comparable to Moloi's: he wanted to preserve Swazi custom and ritual and pagan beliefs in the face of the modern world, while at the same time trying to enjoy the benefits of Western economic vigour. It's not possible. Western culture, and Western economics, do not stop at the threshold of the family home. For better or for worse they come crowding in. Only extreme poverty and isolation can protect a culture, and that is a trade-off nobody seems to recommend to their own people.

As I was leaving Godfrey Moloi's club, I asked him about a picture of Pik Botha and F.W. de Klerk displayed prominently in the entrance. He sighed. He understood that he was asking for trouble. This picture can be seen in two ways: either he misses the certainties of the old order, or he feels compelled to pour cold water on the one nation concept. Either way, a less prudent gesture could not be imagined.

Leaving Soweto, my guide directed me down a narrow back street. Soweto is a place where anonymity is writ large: the streets have no names and the houses look as though they were delivered by truck. Some youths (the word in South Africa is fraught with varying degrees of menace) were sauntering in the middle of the road. They showed no signs of moving; I slowed down.

'Don't slow down.'

'Why not?'

'Just drive at them.'

'What if I hit someone?'

'That's his problem.'

At the last moment they moved out of the way. I wondered if Soweto could ever be drawn into the communality of South African life. Rugby, according to Moloi, meant nothing here. The whole World Cup was a white man's fiesta. Yet my guide, Mashodane, told me that many blacks had become interested in the World Cup.

I was back in South Africa. You could believe any damn thing as the mood took you.

Chapter 8

When I talked to Nadine Gordimer again some days later, I mentioned my conversation with Moloi. As a determinist, she is inclined to see people like him as irrelevant or out of touch. The feeling I had at times was that any number of people in South Africa were, by this measure, irrelevant. We filmed her again in the sitting-room of her house. She was warm and welcoming and had read two of my books in the year that had passed. I, by contrast, felt dispirited. I could think of nothing new to ask her, although I started to go through the motions. She told me that the battle for the independent funding of the arts was over. Arts councils would be set up and each region would have an arts minister. Andries Oliphant and Mike van Graan, with the help of Njabula Ndebele when required, had swung the argument away from those who favoured government control of the arts. In less than a year the widely predicted threat of cultural commissars was no more. And Mongane Wally Serote, Nadine's friend and potential arts dictator, was now in parliament. He had written some new poetry, which hinted at the difficulties of the idea of home for the exiles.

Gordimer has often talked about the notion of home. She has said, and she repeated for the camera, that she sees her writing partly as a process of making sense of her role in South Africa, of finding a home. Now, she confirmed, she could truly claim she was home. It had taken her years to see that Europe, and specifically England, was not home. Her parents spoke of England as home, although her father was a Latvian Jew. As a girl she imagined she had been born outside the real world in the dreary mining town of Springs. It took her many years to discover that this was the real world, and that her job was to find and define her place in it.

As she was talking, diligently answering my lacklustre questions, I began to grow excited. Yes, I thought, home and culture are the higher truths to which she is so clearly in thrall. And I am a rootless person, living in Islington, sneering at the popular culture of Britain, sceptical about the possibility of one nation in South Africa. It wasn't altogether unpleasurable, because there is some satisfaction in imagining oneself to have no illusions.

She told me that although a great deal had been achieved the country was now in a dangerous and difficult period, the period of transition, and she cited Flaubert. I thought of Milton talking about Oliver Cromwell, whom I had studied at Oxford: 'Peace hath her victories, no less renowned.' But I also knew that I could never be like Gordimer: I could envy her, and the symmetry of her life and work, but I felt, despite her protestations that she had never confused her political role – 'the essential gesture' of Barthes – with propaganda, that it was not so easy to make the distinction.

Since first meeting her a year ago I had reread, and in some cases read for the first time, many of her books. Christopher Hope had once complained of the heavy-handed sententiousness of her writing, but I found instead a strong thread of rationalism. Everything must have a purpose and an explanation. In her attempts to define herself and her role, she has perhaps tethered herself too close to the ground. Her prose never soars away, because it is attached by a thin filament of rationality which runs through everything she does and says, so that almost every character and situation has a relevance, sometimes a surfeit of relevance. But then, writers who have no close identification with social issues and no location in sites of historical significance are unlikely to win the Nobel prize.

After filming she invited me into the dining-room for a drink as the crew packed up. She and Reinhold were about to eat roast chicken, prepared down the corridor by her noiseless, amiable servants. As a teenager, I once produced my own meat pie at dinner as a protest against our having servants. Now I have a nostalgia for the colonial life, as we lived it, for sensible food and smiling servants and clubs where chitties were signed.

It was growing dark outside, with the chill of a Johannesburg winter still in the air. This chill is like an invisible mist rising from the ground. I wished I could stay for dinner but the crew were ready to go. I left her again, busy, bright, and set out through the leafy streets where I had been brought up, back to the more recent and flashier suburbs to the north. As I drove away, I remembered meeting a genuine nymphomaniac, right on the corner of Frere Road. She stepped off a bus and smiled at me. Reading Gordimer's work again, I had seen that she placed a great deal of importance on sex as a motor of human activity. In a sense I think she finds the irrationality of the sexual motive a respite from rationality. But she also warns about prurience in reading novels: she quotes Edward Said, that the writer implies but withholds the actual events of his life: 'Art is the interpreter of the human world.' But her novels suggest a sensual attachment to the struggle as well as an ideological one. As we drove down the familiar streets, I took comfort in that.

In *Burger's Daughter* she made a fictional account of the life of Bram Fischer, and a homage to him and his family. She says in a recent book that one of her most precious moments was receiving confirmation that the novel was a true picture of his life. From this I think it is reasonable to conclude that being true to the struggle and, in that sense, its leaders, is high on her list of priorities. So she will never be free from the curiosity about the connection between her novels and what has happened in South Africa. She is no mere chronicler of events, but a major figure. Such is her celebrity that she was off to Cannes as a judge at the film festival. The question I pondered, however, is whether Bram Fischer ever wondered about the essentially illiberal nature of communism, or indeed any of the closed systems of belief. Doris Lessing has described recently her revulsion for communism when she realised what Stalin was up to. It's not really a question of Stalin's mad sadism, but of the whole notion of the quasi-scientific account of human nature and governance. And I detect in Nadine Gordimer something of that historicism still lingering on and to some extent hindering her writing.

In the restaurant we heard that Will Carling, the England captain, had been reinstated after being suspended for calling the English rugby administrators 'old farts'. Just before I left for South Africa I had interviewed his manager, who told me that the problem with English rugby was that it was run by old farts. In the restaurant we discussed rugby and ate Greek *meze* followed by grilled squid. I thought of Nadine and Reinhold eating their roast chicken in the long and sombre dining-room. There is nothing you could tell Gordimer about the relationship, and its attendant ironies, between masters and servants, or more commonly in the local parlance, madams and maids. As Democratic MP Peter Soal told me, during the election one of his constituents had driven to the polling station with her maid and asked him where black people voted. South Africa is full of small ironies.

But the bigger irony is this: while the outside world was losing interest in what white South Africans have to say, at home Mongane Wally Serote's suggestion that whites learn to listen was still not being heeded. Everywhere in the negotiating process and in the negotiation about the arts I saw a central paradox: there's no such thing as an African aesthetic and political point or precept which is clearly distinguishable from the liberal, Western point of view. Even in such matters as tolerance of the South African Communist Party, headed since the death of Joe Slovo by my old friend Essop Pahad, there is no clear Africanist way of looking at this. Essentially you either believe that the Communist Party is a good thing, because you are a Stalinist, or you believe it is not, because you are a Social Democrat. In the arts, you either believe that the Party and the government should make all decisions, or you believe that independent bodies should be set up. Neither side of either of these related arguments can be said to have an African perspective, and herein lies a dilemma for South Africa: what are Africans bringing to the argument? I say this not because I think they should bring something unique, but because they think they should, and because people like Gordimer think they should. *Ubuntu*, or common humanity, is one such notion. The reading of history favoured in progressive circles is that African peoples lived in harmony or *ubuntu* until the white man arrived. So even the evident distaste of traditional Zulus for the new dispensation goes back to white interference. And of course it is unequivocally true that whites disrupted (and often destroyed) every single community with which they came into contact. And it could be argued that the Inkatha Zulus are really no more than those Zulus who were trapped beyond the Buffalo River by British colonialism.

On 10 May 1994, Mandela famously said, 'Wat is verby is verby' – what is past, is past. The problem now, once the big issues have lost their shine, is to find a basis for common values. In truth this is not a problem unique to South Africa. The attribution of value is a tricky philosophic and political dilemma in all societies. In South Africa there is a belief that in black life and black culture lies something uniquely valuable. But either the old ways were destroyed irreparably and *ubuntu* was damaged beyond repair, or there was never a culture or an aesthetic which was applicable to the conditions of life as it is now lived. Wittgenstein said trying to salvage damaged traditions is like trying to repair a spider's web with your bare hands.

South Africa today, it seemed to me, was going along blindly (blinded in part by the good fortune of having

Mandela as a leader) in a direction it had not fully investigated. What would happen when the facts of the Third Force were made public? What about the informers, torturers and murderers within the liberation movement? Their story is not pleasant either, nor are the events surrounding the death of Stompie Moeketsi. It occurred to me, as we ate our Mediterranean food, that the only people who were above suspicion, who could reasonably claim to be clean, were those who had been in prison for twenty-seven years. And perhaps, I thought, there is a perverse advantage in having ideals which have been nurtured and fostered in prison, away from the realities of politics. What Mandela had brought from prison to South Africa was the sense of the nobility of political struggle. Unbending, unswervingly loyal to the cause, but a cause whose main objective was always seen to be the toppling of white minority rule.

What now? Play rugby, build houses, develop culture, encourage 'democracy'? And at the end of the process – if there is an end – what sort of society is coming? Just as I didn't believe that Soweto would ever become part of the communality of South Africa, so I wondered if the past could ever really be forgotten. When, for example, the people of Soweto begin to ask why things have not changed, the more opportunistic politicians will say, as Godfrey Moloi was suggesting, that those in power have sold out to the whites. The onion peeling will begin. Whites will be blamed for all shortcomings and apartheid for all imbalances. The economy will collapse, and this will prove conclusively that white capitalism is loaded against Africans. And yet Van Zyl Slabbert had told me that the South African settlement was simply a deal. I kept remembering his words. He approved of that because it was based on a common interest and compromise. It is in fact Hobbesian.

But what are the values which South Africa is going to cherish, and in what way may they be described as African? The values which South Africa now espouses officially owe a great deal to British liberalism and its followers like Sol

Plaatje. His spiritual descendants, who include Mandela, are still in thrall to this tradition. I see no philosophical problem in this; after all, ideas are universal, but there is a sense in which it is an alien tradition, which leaves the door open for nationalism and Afro-centrism.

If Johannesburg, a year from the election, was still tense, I detected a little bravado too. People told me you had to be careful, as though they had been wised up. I have heard it said in Northern Ireland that the distinction of being somewhere that was in the news and the ever-present threat of violence was a stimulant. Peace brought deflation of the spirits in some quarters. Johannesburg seemed to me to be thriving on fear and tension. It made many people believe that they were living in a distinctive place, the murder capital of the world. Here at Bellini's, two girls with very big hair – gigantic hair – were using a cellphone alternately. I thought about identity in South Africa. I guessed that these girls, so blithely South African, were unaware of Nadine Gordimer in the older, more staid part of town, and her life's work. It was as if the suburbs trickled away from the town into amnesia.

And maybe, I thought, South Africans will be saved by their amnesia.

Chapter 9

I had been given a letter written by Fatima Meer decrying the funding of the National Symphony Orchestra by the SABC. Anyone familiar with the BBC's cultural revolution would understand the logic of this letter perfectly: first, she wondered how the governors could justify supporting this minority interest above all other forms of music, for instance indigenous music. Second, she used a specious argument about its disproportionate cost in the budget. And third, there was a hint of menace in her clinching remarks, that while she herself enjoyed its music, it was not up to the politically enlightened, like herself, to connive in its funding. The letter was so shot through with illogicality and that apparent correctness by which the politically motivated impose their will, that I felt it boded ill for the SABC. Worse, for a governor and a biographer, it was full of grammatical mistakes.

The new director of the SABC, Zwelakhe Sisulu, whom I had interviewed briefly a year before when he was the heir apparent, was now installed on the seventeenth floor, with a glorious view north towards Pretoria. He occupied the office at the top of the building built by the Broederbond-dominated SABC in the seventies in its expansionist phase. It was going to use television to continue the policy of apartheid. There would be programmes suited to all races but, in some way the SABC would be able to control, directed only at those races. The madness of this policy became apparent when the first of the imported programmes was screened and showed, despite continual censorship, that there were parts of the world where apartheid did not apply. And advertisers quickly became adept at suggesting a new world where commercial considerations were more important than race. I am sure that advertising was, like sport, a huge factor in the freeing of the South African mind.

From his seventeenth-floor office Zwelakhe Sisulu could look northwards. (Afrikaners, since the Great Trek of 1838, were angled northwards towards unbounded space, just as Muslims are inclined towards Mecca.) On a good day Sisulu can probably see the Voortrekker Memorial in Pretoria. On the other side of the road lies the Johannesburg Country Club. As we set up to film, I looked down on the scene of many of my teenage revels. The swimming-pool beside the giant oak tree, where toasted sandwiches were served, was azure. The grounds, which to us were so English with their herbaceous borders and rolling lawns (brown at this time of the year), I realised now, were impossibly lush with constant watering and sunshine, the plants almost obscenely vigorous. The golf course had long ago been appropriated by the Rand Afrikaans University, leaving only two holes, but the cricket field, with a tree quaintly at mid-wicket, was still there. History moves at high speed in South Africa. The Country Club, once English, had first been infiltrated by Afrikaners from the SABC, and was now increasingly multiracial. Sisulu was detained, as were his father and his brother, and now he was ensconced in this not too tasteful suite, high above the murder capital of the world, looking down incidentally on the site of some of my minor conquests and concomitant disappointments.

To be brought up in South Africa is to be very conscious of race. Since our last meeting, I had become aware that the Sisulus were not entirely African. Zwelakhe has a curious complexion, slightly mottled, and a sparse beard. His secretary was a glowingly white Afrikaans girl, and she had told me how wonderful he was. Many people say this about the whole Sisulu clan. They radiate an unmistakable generosity of spirit and decency.

I reminded Sisulu of our conversation of a year ago and his claim that he would be able to handle any pressure from the ANC. A few days before, Thabo Mbeki had suggested that the government be given half an hour each week to speak for itself. 'Thabo's half hour' had been ridiculed and the suggestion was withdrawn. All politicians, in my experience, are tempted to use the public broadcaster. Sisulu seemed to be amused by the incident. I asked him if it was true that he had been subjected to pressures. Nothing untoward, he said. Would it not be possible that the aristocracy of the ANC, the Mandelas, Sisulus and Mbekis, would be inclined to expect favours from each other? After all, they were an exceptionally powerful faction in the new South Africa, even the maverick Winnie, who was then Deputy Minister of Arts, Science and Technology. These sons of the great men, I thought, now in early middle age, were bound to be on the phone to each other. He didn't deny either that there was an aristocracy or that they were close, but he denied that he was likely to bend in their direction. In fact he was involved that week in a presentation to the IBA, to outline his notion of public service broadcasting and his proposals for the future. Television and radio at that time, May 1995, were in chaos, with Monty Pythonesque incompetence on display on every channel. But Sisulu explained that the visible and audible outputs were designed to reflect the cultural and racial composition of the country. The result was appalling and soon began to be reconsidered. It was clear that whatever 'One nation, many cultures' meant, it did not make for clear and comprehensible broadcasting if all these cultures were jostling each other in every programme.

There was a burden of expectation, said Sisulu, which came from the culture of resistance. The culture of resistance assumed that things could be changed simply and quickly, as in warfare. I asked him about the one nation concept. It was not his job to impose cultural values, but in his analysis the nation had wanted to unify but had been kept apart. (How often I heard this observation, and how often I wondered exactly what it meant.) But Sisulu was confident that a dynamic young culture would emerge as the nation fused. I asked him about any possible threats to the National Symphony Orchestra (armed as I was with Fatima Meer's letter). He said there was no threat, but of course instruments which were associated with classical music could be used to play African music. We are, he said, a hybrid society.

As regards the funding of the arts, the SABC was expected to make a contribution to the debate but had not yet had time. It wasn't long before the climactic arts debate was to take place, but he was too concerned with the changes that were taking place and the strains on the system. The standards to which I referred – not themselves very high – were the standards of the white élite and did not reflect society. This was almost exactly the argument that Gordimer had used. It seemed to me to suggest that Eurocentricity would be used as a defence more and more often in the future. As for Winnie Mandela, he praised her energy but felt that in making her a minister there had been inadequate understanding. She would be back and more mature. I wondered how he could be so sanguine. If Emma Gilbey is correct, Zwelakhe's mother was present when two gunmen murdered Abubaker Asvat on Winnie's orders.

Sisulu agreed that the SABC would be crucial in the shaping of the new South African cultural identity. He used the word 'reflect' a number of times. The broadcasting service must reflect the new South Africa. I wondered if it would reflect belief in ritual murder amongst the Venda or Godfrey Moloi's view that Soweto was soon to explode. I doubted it. Public service broadcasting is a difficult if admirable notion, depending in the end on oligarchy in the boardroom. And the board of the SABC, as exemplified by Fatima Meer, was determinedly ANC. For all that, I found Sisulu to be a man of wide understanding and – yes – generous vision. Compared with the desperate crowd of brown-suited professors and dokters who controlled the SABC in the old regime, Sisulu appeared to have come from another, more sophisticated, universe. As I had noted long ago, many of the leaders of the ANC have a cosmopolitanism entirely lacking in the National Party. The reason, I guess, was that they had looked outside the country for their philosophical props. And, of course, many of them had actually lived outside the country for long periods.

We filmed some training courses for would-be directors and producers. An actor was making menacing gestures at the camera, which either zoomed in close or stayed out at a safe distance. The trainees were asked to comment on the effect. One woman said that the close-ups were good for humorous programmes. The only white man looked uneasy, trying to join in the attractive, new African openness. But perhaps I only imagined his unease.

Late in the afternoon we drove to a former mine dump on the edge of the city. Here the father of my good friend Ruargh Findlay had pioneered the conversion of mine dumps into real estate. He covered this one with topsoil, planted grass, and called it Park Central. At one point he had a swimming pool and offices way up there and we sometimes used to be allowed to play. But these enterprises never flourished. The Top Star Drive-In, which was probably the first and last drive-in to be built on a slag heap (actually yellow, unhealthy-looking waste from the gold extraction process), was now abandoned, although the screen and the projection rooms and some other evidence of its former life still existed. The reverse of the screen supported a huge neon sign, which lit up as we set our camera down to film some scenics of the city.

As in the American West, the end of the day in South Africa, particularly up here in the Highveld, can usually be relied upon to produce spectacular sunsets, when the lights of buildings down in the gloom contrast with the bands of orange, white and blue, just like the old flag, above. Sometimes these sunsets suddenly catch fire, the clouds incandescent from the glow of the departed sun. This one, to be truthful, was muted, but still Johannesburg below – tall buildings now pointillist, cars zipping by on the freeway, the sky becoming pink and azure – looked wonderfully raw and alive. But we had put our camera right in the pathway from the city. As the sun went down a stream of people arrived from below, like sherpas in a never-ending procession. They were living in the old projection room and the kitchen from where the waiters in their little American sailor hats used to set out with trays of hamburgers, root beer and fries, always accompanied by an enormous wagon-wheel of tomato and crudely chopped lettuce, which we threw out of the window. The ketchup was tinny and unnaturally coloured. I hardly need to say that the windows were steamed up and watching the flicks, as we called them, was quite low on our list of priorities.

Against the background of a darkening sky I interviewed the director and actor John Matshikiza. In fact he was brought up in Zambia and in England. I had filmed him the previous year directing *Julius Caesar* and I asked him now how it had gone. Well, he said, during its short run. I was to see, however, that there was a problem with these productions: the limited numbers who came were largely still white, and many of them were not in the mood to support theatre which had a political message, particularly if the message was none too favourable to whites. Not because they disagreed with this general analysis, but because they were the liberal few who had supported liberation and supported the theatre and did not want simplistic criticism when they paid to go out. And run the risk of having the BMW hijacked into the bargain.

Matshikiza was dismissive of Johannesburg's culture. There was very little appreciation of books, cinema, theatre, graphics or the plastic arts. He said it was a cowboy culture, quick to latch on to the most superficial subjects and themes, but reluctant to look closely at anything. His series on Africa was an example: he had tried to show South Africans that

Africa was not just famine and disaster, but vibrant, creative and an inspiration. He feared an American blandness which was probably the result of isolation. For all that, he had read Roy Campbell complaining in the forties of the lack of curiosity of South Africans. (Campbell, William Plomer and Laurens van der Post had wanted in their journal *Voorslag* 'to sting with satire the bovine hindquarters of the Union'.) It struck me, however, that there was a logical inconsistency in this complaint. In the forties South African society was white and hardly took any notice of blacks. Roy Campbell, whose embrace of fascism denied him the recognition that is now his due, was not the poet of Africa but of an isolated group of whites with artistic inclinations. Was Matshikiza complaining that the whites lacked curiosity, or was he saying that the whole society, black and white, lacks curiosity? Too much energy was being dissipated in discussion of these issues rather than in creativity, he said. He was also sceptical of the idea of a new cultural identity. Because it had been illegal to think, nobody was any longer capable of thinking, of making the deep philosophic investigation required. For him, this would start with the examination of the past and the stories of the leaders. He felt that fiction could be made out of Robben Island, for example, which would provide an enormous resource. It seemed a lame conclusion to me, particularly as one of the best plays ever to come out of South Africa is Fugard's *The Island*. Yet his general thesis, that isolation and – I am interpolating – lack of education had produced an inarticulacy and deficiency of awareness, I found all too believable.

Down there, under the slag heap, was Dryden's Engineering. I could see the sign clearly. Dryden's son had been a friend of mine, too. I had this thought: all over the world I have known people and had friends, and yet in some ways my lost friends of my teenaged years in this makeshift city were dearer to me than the others. Without realising it, I had probably, like Nadine Gordimer, found a home here.

There were food stalls down below the Top Star where the

buses and taxis congregated, selling chicken curry and chips and sausages and pap or porridge, but I would never dream of eating there. Why not? In Singapore I have eaten greedily at the open-air stalls. In Turkey by the roadside and market side you could not keep me away. Why not Africa, my own home? Why can't I go and eat a grilled mealie, or *wors en pap* from a roadside vendor? Because I believe I will become ill at worst or be disgusted by overcooked chicken flesh and sausages full of gristle. But I don't know. Instead I ate among the affluent and extravagantly coiffed of Johannesburg's white suburbs each evening, remembering what Godfrey Moloi had said about killing a sheep. Once in northern Kenya the Samburu camel drivers had killed a goat and offered me a small piece of freshly cooked liver, an honour, or at least a courtesy. I swallowed it. It was fine. But I would have preferred it in a sauce of balsamic vinegar and caramelised onions on a bed of fashionable, slightly bitter leaves. In French Africa, I am told you can eat extraordinarily well. I wondered about the cultural constructs, so easily dismissed in considering the future of societies. I remembered, too, a book I had been reading which attributed the persistence of irrational thought – of which of course we are all guilty daily, even hourly – to this fact, that the brain was determined to make meaning of the great unknowable, namely death. All societies at all times, the writer suggested, have had to come up with explanations of nothingness, and these explanations essentially are the basis of all religion.

That night we had dinner in the Russian Tearooms beside the Land Rover sales room back in the northern suburbs. The restaurant, looking a little bit but not much like the real article in Manhattan, is next to the Land Rovers priced at £90,000. I ate – I have noted it in my diary – Cape salmon followed by blinis. I was to eat there a few more times too, huddled in this pleasant but make-believe Russian restaurant, without a black face visible, apart from the security men outside.

The next day we were to film the Soweto String Quartet.

They had released a record, *Zebra Crossing*, which pictured them wearing zebra-skin jackets. We caught up with them filming a video in the zoo, near the zebra enclosure. On closer inspection, the jackets seemed to be rather tawdry. Sandile Khemese and I spoke. He was doing well and the record was a big success, he said. A party of black schoolchildren was shepherded by. They wore gymslips and neat shirts and trousers, but they were much louder and more confident than black children would have been a few years before. The director of the video got the playback going and asked the Soweto Quartet to play along: 'Do something vibey' was his exact instruction to Sandile, who bowed away stoically. The zebra in the background were puzzled at first and milled closer to the camera, but they soon lost interest. We left the director trying, in that way which plagues all film endeavours, to line up the satisfying shot, in this case the feverish quartet in their ill-fitting zebra jackets, and the delicate zebra with the short attention spans. This demanded crab-like movements by the quartet as the zebra migrated round their enclosure.

Nigel Williams, author of *The Wimbledon Poisoner*, and also the editor of my BBC programme, had imagined that things in South Africa would quickly become anarchic and interesting after the elections. I felt a duty to try to find examples of this sort of thing, but in truth I was finding not so much anarchy as a strange unreality. Everything had changed but people, both black and white, were still waiting to see what this meant. Some, like Godfrey Moloi, expected nothing. Others, like the Soweto String Quartet, were looking forward to wealth and acclaim. Whereas a few years before they would have had trouble with their passes in this area, they were now allowed to agitate the zebra with the good wishes of the Zoological Society. I doubt if they, in common with most black people in South Africa, had seen a zebra in its natural habitat.

Nobody knew what was going to happen. The whites were sublimating their worries in eager anticipation of the Rugby World Cup. But it seemed to me that the enormity of what had come about was causing unease. The strangeness of South Africa, masked by apartheid, was coming into view. I remembered once seeing a whale beached and being amazed at the massive, encrusted body so unexpectedly exposed. I remembered Godfrey Moloi's image of doves released at midnight.

Chapter 10

There were two Shakespeare productions in May 1995, two that I knew of anyway. One was Welcome Msomi's Zulu *Macbeth*, *Umabatha*, and the other was Antony Sher's *Titus Andronicus*. The Zulu *Macbeth* was playing at the Civic Theatre, a large building set in a dead zone of landscaped grass and artful fountains. (My father, incidentally, had a part in raising the subscription for one of these fountains, a statue of heroic miners which sprayed water.) Culture in South Africa used to produce this rictus, this sacerdotal nervousness, because culture was a serious business, and also guilt-inducing. You dressed up for culture in order to placate it.

We filmed a final rehearsal and watched the opening night of *Umabatha*. It was stunning. When Duncan (Dingane) and his party went to visit the Macbeths, I felt that tingle of excitement which is supposed to affect the hairs on the back of one's neck, but in fact is more like a mild convulsion of the whole system. The music, the dancing and the costumes evoked directly a medieval savagery and splendour in a way that I had never seen before. Lady Macbeth's exhortations to her husband, her spine stiffening, produced an unexpected reaction in the audience: they laughed. In fact some women sitting near me on opening night were beside themselves. It was clear that the notion of strong women and vacillating men had great appeal. Msomi told me that women in traditional Zulu society are indeed strong and resourceful. The audience recognised that women, despite the posturing of men, were pulling the strings. It seemed to me, if proof were needed, that Shakespeare was instantly recognisable. These were not events taking place a long time ago in Scotland, but Zulu dynastic struggles which were very immediate. And as I write this, I think of the Venda and their fondness for poisoning and witchcraft. The three witches were dressed as *sangomas*, sometimes called witch-doctors by the politically unenlightened, and Msomi had had a hundred *sangomas* file on to the stage at Mandela's inauguration, so making it clear that he, at least, recognised that they were a part of African culture. The appeal of Shakespeare, I thought, might also owe something to the fact that, as Harold Bloom puts it, 'he has no theology, no metaphysics, no ethics, and rather less political theory than is brought to him by his current critics'.

I talked to Msomi about the past year. He said that the inauguration of Mandela, with two thousand performers, was undoubtedly the highlight of his whole career. Though he had coined the phrase 'One nation, many cultures', he believed that progress in that direction would come largely from individual efforts, and that it would take time, but he said that there was (and I was very aware of this) a powerful urge to forge a new identity. What this was precisely, he seemed to be leaving up to market and creative forces. But he had found that there were plenty of opportunities in the theatre. There was enormous interest in *Umabatha* and the audience was coming from all sections of the population, he said, and the opening night a few days later was, as I have said, riotous. Here, I thought, in this exuberant, optimistic and quite prosperous audience, lay the future of South Africa, in a sort of feel-good culture.

The contrast with the other Shakespeare going on at the Market Theatre, not a mile down the road, was revealing. Antony Sher was staging a production of *Titus Andronicus*, heavily signposted as being of significance for South Africa.

The Market is a very distinguished theatre, as everyone knows, but its place in the new South Africa is far from assured. First I detected a certain revulsion for the issues of the past; the self-lacerating phase which had brought about a revival of theatre and a new understanding of the importance of theatre in the polemic was considered to be, in some subtle ways, best forgotten. And second, there was a wariness about making the trip to downtown Johannesburg at night. The Market crouches under the expressway in an area which, while it is being reclaimed for art, still has a forgotten and desolate aspect, the sort of thing one sees in American cities like Detroit. Johannesburgers, I thought again, believe they have done their stuff: they want to be entertained and flattered now. Sher's production was playing to audiences of less than fifty. He had written a piece in one of the papers suggesting that South Africans had lost interest in art; they had no curiosity about the outside world, and the cultural boycott, which he had supported vigorously, had encouraged a parochial mentality.

I interviewed him in his dressing-room before he went on. Outside an actress was doing voice exercises, howling and groaning. The dressing-room was smaller than many broom-cupboards, separated by a curtain from the next one. I could imagine that these mean and cramped circumstances would have appealed to the pioneering spirit in a great actor if the production was a success, but it was a huge flop.

As he applied his make-up, Sher's face was extraordinary. His short hair was bleached and he had grown a chin beard, so that he looked as though he had been caught in a dilemma: the top two-thirds of his face were taut, strained and, in that urban way, gay, while the bottom third was Old Testament and prophetic. On top of the short hair he wore a military beret when he went on, so that to the other conflicting images contained within one face, a jaunty Montgomery of Alamein element was added. The intention, of course, was to draw a parallel with the AWB, the know-nothing, far right wing of South African politics, and its absurd leader, Eugene

Terreblanche. Although Sher was to tell me that in Britain people were used to modern-dress, or completely random-dress, Shakespeare, and did not require a classical interpretation – what he called 'wrinkly-tights Shakespeare' – I couldn't help thinking that many of the modern-dress productions I have seen make superficial points and shallow analogies that only actors and directors find rewarding. A recent production of *The Merchant of Venice* in Stratford compared the Rialto to the City of London in the eighties. Not a bad comparison on the physical level, but on the deeply troublesome questions it was no help at all.

Sher admitted to being disappointed by the response to his production. He was getting no black audiences for reasons of cash, transport and crime. But what puzzled him most was this lack of curiosity. The RSC had passed through earlier and had had a poor response too. The only happy aspect of the whole production, he said, was the opportunity to work with South African actors who were exceptionally good. (All the while the actress was groaning and keening just outside.)

Was it a mistake, I wondered, to do it with a variety of Afrikaans accents? His reply was that English as spoken in Shakespeare's day was far from middle-class English, 'the accent that I am using now'. I found this remark interesting, because it confirmed a sense that we South Africans have, however well integrated, a habit of assuming modes of speech and mind when we live abroad. We have a changeable sense of home – I was becoming increasingly taken with this notion – a place which no longer exists, I thought, but might have. Nadine Gordimer was confident that it existed, but to me it was as mythological as ever, composed of historical and racial oddments and – as I now realised – wholly arbitrary identification with the landscape. Sher gave an example of how Shakespearean actors would have spoken the word 'war'. He let out a kind of Celtic growl, which for a moment silenced the voice limbering exercises outside, and which he said sounded just like Afrikaans. Whatever it sounded like, it was a reminder of this tense, calculated actor's great power.

Theatre, he said, should be nourishing. The problem with actors, as with many contemporary painters, I thought, is that they regard any damn thing they are involved with as nourishing for the rest of us. The truth is we often want to see actors and artists show us their skills, not their critiques of society or reappraisals of the art forms in which they are engaged.

I asked him if people were resentful of him. I had heard that he was not highly regarded, but then it is a characteristic of all provincial places to be ambivalent about their departed sons and daughters. He said that some whites had said, 'You've come back now, now that South Africa is chic' (which in South Africa is pronounced 'chick'), but blacks were welcoming, knowing that he had worked for Anti Apartheid.

I don't think South Africans, white or black, realise what a great actor they have in Sher. But in their desire to see wrinkly-tights Shakespeare, rather than in-your-face Shakespeare, I recognised not just nostalgia for pre-apartheid times, as Sher suggested, but a desire for normality. Why should they now get a heavily loaded Shakespeare? Up the road, produced by Welcome Msomi, was the perfect Shakespeare for the times, vigorous, colourful and glamorous, with a far more appealing parallel than the one this *Titus Andronicus* was offering. *Umabatha* was the Shakespeare that corresponded to known reality in South Africa, as the war between Inkatha and the ANC was going on.

Sher went on in his Sam Browne and beret atop a Land Rover pulled by his supporters. I thought it was striking and moving, but I have to admit I had never seen *Titus Andronicus*, and I now understood why it was disinterred so infrequently. Although Sher was very good, his Afrikaans accent was far from authentic, and I longed for him to rip it away and give us the great, actorish delivery of which he was capable. In the end Shakespeare's characters, not some imposed interpretation, must be given primacy. Hegel said that Shakespeare's uniqueness was that the characters can contemplate themselves objectively as works of art. The audience was being asked to contemplate not the characters so much as a glib analogy.

That evening I heard for the first time the South African song for the coming World Cup, 'Shosholoza', originally a Zimbabwean song celebrating the return home of migrant workers by steam train, *Istimela*. As a schoolboy at Bishops in Cape Town, I had travelled eight times a year the thousand miles by steam train, for nine years. We travelled second class, near to the engine. The only people who got more cinders in their eyes than us were the migrant blacks in third class, right behind the engine. As I heard 'Shosholoza' on the car radio, I had suddenly powerful recollections of these journeys which I had all but forgotten. Nine times eight thousand miles. I had travelled seventy-two thousand miles by steam train, by *Istimela*. I could remember jumping off at Kimberley for fish and chips and I could remember the tedium of the Karoo, dotted with inquisitive meerkats, and the breakfasts at 1/6d which sustained us on the thirty-six-hour journey. What amazed me, as it came back, was the thought of the contrast between the way we were treated as boys and the solicitous way I have behaved towards my own sons. Aged nine, I travelled eight thousand miles in one year, found my way from the station in Cape Town to the local train, and hauled my luggage up the road to the hated boarding-house. Nobody met us; nobody welcomed us; nobody inquired after our welfare. Yes, I thought, 'Shosholoza' is my song too; I was a migrant worker. And in this way, I realised, many South Africans are rediscovering their past. Some are inventing it, others are reshaping it.

I went to bed in the bland hotel which stood on the site of a nursery out in Sandton. We'd lived near here when my father was first appointed editor of the *Rand Daily Mail*. We used to ride our ponies here on dirt roads, disturbing guinea-fowl and small deer. There was a reminder of those days down at the river which is distinctly African, the rocks granite-hard, the water dangerously unpredictable. After a summer flood, debris would be left high in trees. Here we splashed about and played at building dams and once my reluctant father, in a wholly uncharacteristic act, drowned some unwanted kittens here. He said the barbel would eat them. Barbel were supposed to taste of mud, but nobody ever caught them. On another occasion our gardener – known as the 'garden boy' – was late for work, and apologised briefly. He and his friend had been attacked crossing the river, and his friend, sadly, was dead.

I was thinking about Shakespeare. Is it true that Shakespeare, as Sol Plaatje, who translated Shakespeare into Tswana maintained, appeals instantly to all cultures without mediation, essentially what Harold Bloom was to claim in *The Western Canon*? Put another way, are art and culture universal? Shakespeare is art. Art is truth. As Emmanuel Levinas expresses it, 'Art does not know a particular type of reality.' (In fairness, I should add that Levinas does not absolve artists of social responsibility.) Art doesn't need special pleading or editing. I couldn't make up my mind: was the Zulu *Macbeth* a success because it was a cracking story – Duncan's terrific fervour and panache in Zulu – or was it a success because of the universality of Shakespeare's characters and the chance we have to contemplate ourselves in them?

Before I fell asleep I made a note of this question because it seemed to me significant in South Africa. I remembered, too, what Zwelakhe Sisulu had said about the National Symphony Orchestra, that it should learn to play African music on its instruments. Is this really possible, except as a gesture? Was the whole notion of hybridising the culture ('We're a hybrid nation,' Zwelakhe had said) a contradiction in terms? And although I could not make up my mind before I slept, I wondered, was the notion of one culture no more than a metonymy for an inexpressible hope?

Now, as I write, I think that this idea of culture as a figure of speech for hope is identical to the notion of perfectibility as the keystone of Western culture. Western culture, in its ideal form, strives for truth and perfection. Once you begin to suggest that it is easily adapted to social ends, you have denied its whole purpose. And it is pointless to complain that Western culture is Eurocentric: Western culture is not tied to place or to a specific morality; its contribution to understanding is in its ability to stand outside ideology or religion or place. So the idea that Western culture is of itself oppressive and exclusive is absurd. Nor is Western culture the property of any one group striving for dominance; its scope is the subject of debate in the West just as much as in the developing world.

As I looked at the striving for a cultural identity of the new South Africa, I saw that it was going to be very difficult to separate it from this belief in a struggle for dominance.

Chapter 11

One law for the lion and the ox is oppression. Or: *Freedom for an Oxford don is very different to freedom for an Egyptian peasant.*

The next day we were filming in Alexandra Township. In my mind's eye, I saw the teeming landscape somewhat differently now. Compressed by the camera's lens, this squalid street, with people emerging from the shacks, a bustle of taxis and battered cars, mealies roasting in cooking-oil cans converted to barbecues, innumerable children, busy, brown chickens, a few nibbling cattle and goats; I saw that this was a lively, familiar, even comforting, landscape to the inhabitants.

We had paid three boys who were lounging around on the nearby road to act as protection; the truth is we were worried more by them than any other threats. This road on the outskirts of the township was considered almost suicidal for passing motorists, because of the frequency of hijacks. Mashodane, our security man, kept the Volkswagen bus under close scrutiny. But after we had filmed for a while, I spoke to the boys. None of them had a job. One had worked in a steakhouse briefly, until it had closed. He had Cambridge O-levels and no prospects. These boys, who may, for all I know, have been potential hijackers, could see little future. Freedom for them meant nothing much, except possibly freedom from too close a police scrutiny, exactly what the public were calling for to deal with the rise in crime. As we talked, the most extraordinary sight, a gleaming Rolls Royce, appeared in the long, rolling, chaotic street between the shacks. As he approached our camera, the driver hid his face.

'Gangster?' I asked.

The boys laughed.

'Chauffeur.'

A chauffeur taking a detour to visit a woman or a shebeen, or simply on a family errand, hiding his face in case he should be recognised on this unauthorised excursion. The Rolls Royce was so shiny, so enormously weighty in this insubstantial world of shacks built of corrugated iron and flimsy barriers of barbed wire and bent sticks, and barefoot children with home-made toys, that it was surreal, a reminder that the ox and the lion are lying down together in South Africa. I wondered why the driver was not stoned or the car ripped apart. You could have furnished a couple of shacks sumptuously with the leather seats and the soundless clock and the carpeted floors, but the car glided smoothly and unmolested out of the township towards the northern suburbs. The proximity of Alexandra to the northern suburbs was always a staple of Johannesburg conversation. Separated only by the Pretoria Road from Sandton, the shacks and open drains of Alexandra were an existential puzzle. Why had the place not been moved? Why had it never been cleared up or sanitised? And now, all these years later, despite the John Major-supported cricket field and the University Clinic and some other improvements, it seemed hardly to have changed, except perhaps to have become less easy to ignore, a reproach, and evidence of the deep and possibly fatal divide in this society.

I wondered if this purposeful travelling was affecting my judgement. Was I trying to answer unanswerable questions? Was I trying to make meaning where none was to be had? And was I failing to understand that, for people not making documentaries or writing books, life had simply to be lived?

Later in the day I filmed an elderly man, the father of a

friend, listening to the radio in his town house. My intention was to use this scene to illustrate the incomprehension which the shake-up of the SABC had caused among the traditional radio audience of the English Programme, as it had until recently been called. This charming man, dressed very smartly for the occasion, reminded me so sharply of my father's generation, with its decency and strong sense of propriety, that I was a little ashamed of using him for this purpose. The new South Africa was a mystery to him, a world where 'these chaps' were 'trying to run before they could walk'. These chaps hadn't really been that long out of mud huts; it was asking a bit much of these chaps to expect them to cope with the modern world. To some of these chaps, the light switch was a novelty.

When the time came to say goodbye, our driver, Joseph Madike, clearly expected to have his hand shaken. In the new South Africa, not only are there no inhibitions about shaking hands, there's a mania for it with some gymnastic hand-grips as if camaraderie and togetherness must be demonstrated as often as possible. But this old man simply did not see Joseph. There was nothing deliberately rude or arrogant about this: Joseph was a servant and he was invisible. Later when I told Joe rather guiltily that I felt no insult was intended, he said again that even his own young children did not believe that until a very few years ago he was not allowed to travel without a permit or to go to certain parts of town after dark or to work where he liked or to own property. It was beyond their comprehension. In the same way the old man, who sometimes suggested that he was the product of an aristocratic continental lineage, simply could not comprehend that black people had emerged from the shadows of the white man's fire.

The year before, the Modern Dance Company in Pretoria had given a spectacular performance at President Mandela's inauguration. Now they were holding a workshop in Newtown, the cultural precinct near the Market Theatre. By day the area looked less forbidding, unfinished but very promising, with the huge power station hiding an art gallery in its industrial digestive system, and clusters of buildings old and new, housing cultural workers and cultural organisations. The Modern Dance Company was demonstrating how a work was made. But it was obvious to me that the little girls watching hardly looked as if they were from the ghetto: I raise this quibble because a year before we had heard that opera, ballet and modern dance were reaching out to the townships and rural areas in a drive to take culture where it had never been before. The girls were from a convent in Johannesburg, polyglot certainly, but unmistakably middle-class. The outreach programme in the past year had not reached out very far. My notes say that this was one of the first, possibly even the first, workshop the Modern Dance Company had given. By the time we left the little girls were contracting and pliéing away with enthusiasm. But modern dance at least seemed proof against any criticism about lack of hybridisation; its purpose is just that. The piece they were demonstrating married Indian music with jazz dancing successfully, even triumphantly, and had been played at the inauguration to great acclaim.

Nearby, Rick Burnett runs a gallery specialising in African art. He was the promoter of the woodcarver Jackson Hlungwane, whose work had been recommended to me as an example of previously neglected artistic traditions. I talked to Burnett on the floor of his gallery, sitting in front of some of Hlungwane's woodcarvings – life-size (if we can ever be sure of such a thing) angels. They looked to me like totem-poles or thunderbirds. He said that Jackson Hlungwane was driven by his vision: he was messianic, rather like Blake. He said that Hlungwane teased images out of the wood: Hlungwane understood the language of line, bulk, form, and rhythm. Artspeak is, of course, a specialised jargon, but I would have imagined that in order to be a sculptor you would necessarily have mastered some, or all, of these things. I had heard that Burnett exercised an undue control over

Hlungwane's life, and I put this to him. He said that it had not been an easy relationship, and it had been subject to many misunderstandings. The true relationship was not the one people imagined: Hlungwane regarded Burnett as his servant. Unfortunately there was no sign of the many thousands of rand that Hlungwane had been paid over the years, and this worried him.

How had he discovered Hlungwane, I asked? 'Discovered' was not quite the right word. There had always been a healthy tradition of tribal art, but it was not valued. Burnett had decided that he would go out and view it. He heard about Hlungwane and recognised the quality of his work, just as he had recognised the beauty in South Sotho, Tsonga and Ndebele murals. Burnett saw clearly, he said, the dangers of bringing this work to public attention and, of course, to market: the art was part of a social system. Hlungwane had asked him to sell some of his altars and Burnett had ensured that they went to public exhibitions, as a vital part of South African culture. They were handsomely depicted in a catalogue.

After the camera had stopped running, Burnett asked me if I could find some news of Brandon Hurwitz, a disciple of Hlungwane who was missing, believed to have been killed and his body parts used for tribal medicine. His head, said Burnett, was thought to have been sighted in a refrigerator. His mother was very worried about him, which I thought was understandable. Burnett asked me to contact Warrant Officer Smiley Bezuidenhout of the local police, who was in charge of the case, to see if there was any news. While this was not strictly a cultural matter, it was plain that it could be worked into the film under the guise of cultural relativism. A white boy, I surmised, had gone to live among these people to study at the feet of the master and had fallen foul of the locals. There was probably a sexual element in the puzzle.

Our driver, Joe, was over an hour late for the departure. He had been hijacked in Soweto, the side window of the van broken, but he had managed to escape with the vehicle and, more importantly, with his life. Hijackers in Johannesburg kill the drivers as often as not because the police are too busy to follow up murders without witnesses. Joe was still shocked as we set off for the north, from where he himself came, educated by German missionaries. So it was that I found myself telephoning the witchcraft unit in a small South African town attempting to find Smiley Bezuidenhout. I called from a drive-in café, near a school where beefy, blond white boys, neatly dressed in khaki shorts and shirts and grey pullovers, were playing a game of tag with a tennis ball. We were in the country described by Herman Charles Bosman, from where commandos set off to besiege Baden-Powell at Mafeking, and the men noticed that their leader kept stopping 'kaffirs' to ask them questions; they were impressed by this intelligence-gathering until they discovered that he was asking them only one question, the whereabouts of the road to Mafeking. Many people think that Afrikaners are humourless, particularly in relation to themselves, but Herman Charles Bosman's stories, which I had lately been reading, have a sublime slyness much like Garrison Keillor's. Bosman was a teacher in the area during the thirties. These boys, I thought, were the descendants of his pupils.

At a police station in a nearby town, they knew of Smiley Bezuidenhout. They told me that he was called Smiley because he was so fucking ugly. Louis Trichardt is a town of intense South African-ness with pot-bellied men in shorts, Dutch Reformed churches thrusting their brick steeples skywards, garages servicing tractors in the main street, and an air of menacing quiet. I spoke to an elderly man in a park to get directions. It was the first time in twenty years that I had spoken Afrikaans. He told me that he was something to do with a hunting concession. The German clients would kneel and cry for the soul of the animal they had shot. He seemed to be impressed by the spiritual dimension they brought to hunting. Up until then he had not realised that wildebeest had souls. I remembered a picture of Goering in full Bavarian hunting get-up, designed by himself.

The police station was a substantial collection of buildings. Anyone who is familiar with South Africa finds something disturbing about the official architectural style, usually involving biscuit-coloured bricks and unimaginatively placed windows and doors: no frills, reflecting the no-nonsense attitude within. Official buildings appear to pick up the message of the times unerringly. (I sometimes think television commercials and small ads give an unmediated impression of a country which is more useful than the news bulletins.) Until recently, no black person felt safe even approaching a police station because there was a fair chance that they might not come out again if they ever went in.

I found a policewoman and asked if she knew where Smiley was to be found.

'What's he done?' she asked, seeing the camera.

She was his wife. She led us down a long corridor. Smiley looked like a startled Roy Orbison but not deserving of his advance description by any means. He was prepared to talk about Brandon Hurwitz, but not on camera. He showed me pictures of the missing boy. He looked like one of those faded young people who have taken a lot of hash and lost the thread of things. His hair was in blond rasta dreadlocks. Smiley said that there was no evidence whatsoever to suggest that his head was in a refrigerator somewhere. I thought of asking how many refrigerators there were in Venda, but it seemed too obvious a line of inquiry. Smiley's researches had shown that Brandon Hurwitz had once lived amongst blacks in Soweto. He naturally concluded that you could not expect rational behaviour from such a person. He was sure that Brandon would turn up. I asked him if he had investigated the possibility that he had been murdered because of sexual jealousy, which had been suggested back in Johannesburg. He dealt with me patiently; he had made inquiries but there was no evidence; he had spoken to Brandon's mother.

Smiley was reluctant to be drawn further. His superior, however, was keen to get in on the act. He was eager to tell me, on the record, about ritual murder. The Venda, he said, are a very superstitious people. They sacrifice young girls every year to a white crocodile. (I wonder about the mystique of albino crocodiles, whales, etcetera.) Crocodile brains are a favourite poison. And it's not only his black colleagues who believe they are poisonous. Recently he had sent some crocodile brain samples to the police laboratory in Pretoria for forensic tests. The report from the lab was conclusive: crocodile brains are not toxic. But not all his colleagues are convinced. The men in white coats may not have been aware of the circumstances in which crocodile brains were administered. And anyway, science does not tell the whole story. I was able to sympathise with the last sentiment at least.

This officer was keen to give me chapter and verse of Venda superstition. I imagined that as part of the new South Africa, he had been sent on a course of some sort. He searched around his office in Clouzot-like fashion for the proof and came up with the *Reader's Digest Roadside Guide to South Africa*. He could not find the exact reference, but pointed to a picture of the snake dance as a clincher.

Jackson Hlungwane's home, the New Jerusalem described in Rick Burnett's elegant catalogue, was so run-down and nondescript, perched on what appeared to be a rubbish tip by the side of the road, that I ignored the turn-off. I couldn't believe that a woodcarver and visionary, South Africa's Blake, who must have earned hundreds of thousands of rand (the angels were R7,500 each), would live here in two or three huts; if this was the New Jerusalem of his visions, it certainly was disappointing. But I knew from the catalogues that there was another village a few miles away where he had built altars and other symbolic structures.

I found Jackson Hlungwane sitting on the earth near a fire, hacking away with a small tool at a tree trunk. He is an old man, with an extraordinary, demonic smile and lively eyes. Each deft stroke of the adze – it looked like a small garden hoe – shaped the large log in front of him. Not far off rather desperate disciples were hacking away, to much cruder effect, following the master's very freestyle method. I sat and talked to him through an interpreter. In fact I was keen to get on to the story of Brandon Hurwitz, but I felt that the film demanded an artistic discussion. I had, after all, been told by the professor of fine arts at the Michaelis School of Art in Cape Town that Hlungwane was South Africa's premier woodcarver. Because of the understandable uncertainty about what constitutes art and the awareness that art galleries have reflected an entirely white viewpoint for many years, Jackson Hlungwane's evident skill has made him significant in the eyes of the art establishment. I wanted to see what symbolic importance Hlungwane might have in the traditional world, even though I was aware that the language of art does not always travel. Putting aside all disappointments at the reality of the New Jerusalem, I sat on a tree trunk destined to become one of Hlungwane's angels, and asked about the sources of his inspiration.

He spoke in English with the occasional reference to the interpreter, who was the driver, Joe. What Hlungwane said was largely unintelligible. He talked about heaven and hell and spirits and angels he had seen. He showed me his leg, which was hideously scarred; for some reason he had put it in a fire ten years earlier. This rash act was a source of pride to him. Any attempt to discuss his art unleashed a monologue, animated but repetitious, about heaven and hell and their fusion, in some way which I cannot now recall. He had been to Japan on a cultural visit and showed me some lurid Japanese comics. In one picture he identified himself wearing a crown, and a figure he said was Nelson Mandela, kneeling humbly at his feet. These comics were stored in a hut along with many other memorabilia, including a scrapbook which contained coloured religious pictures with pious captions in French. For each one, Hlungwane had a visionary interpretation. As far as I could see, his art is an expression of his religion. In this sense, it may be very close to the origins of art in all societies. He sees himself as a prophet. The woollen cap on his head, I now realised, was similar to what Rastafarians wear in London. It seemed that South Africa's premier woodcarver was a Rasta! Strangely, I could not recall any mention of his being a Rastafarian in the catalogue. He confirmed that he was indeed a Rasta. In fact he believes himself to be not much lower in the Rasta hierarchy than Haile Selassie. Almost unconsciously he went on chipping away at the tree trunk as we talked. I could see angel features emerging. The wings are done separately, like the wings for a paper aeroplane. In the background his disciples, apparently puzzled by why the outside world placed such a premium on his work, were chopping, chipping, and hacking away. I thought I detected some desperation in their efforts. Hlungwane moved to a smaller piece without warning and flicked delicately at it.

Later we went for a walk by the river to talk about Brandon Hurwitz. I wanted to film him away from the squalid setting of the New Jerusalem, but he had some difficulty walking along the river bank. This river apparently had few crocodiles left – neither of the conventionally coloured nor of the white variety – although the Kruger National Park is only eighty miles away. African rivers are often a muddy brown, as this was, with deep pools and thick reed beds which hint at danger. Hurwitz, said Hlungwane, was his son. He had named him Abel, pronounced 'Aah-bull'. He didn't tell me who Cain was in this scenario, but I wondered if I should tip off Smiley when I saw him again about a new line of inquiry. Hlungwane showed me his hair, releasing from under his tea cosy long dreadlocks which looked like dried moss or lichen. Abel, his adopted son, had been killed, he said, by a local chief. This same man was preventing him from going to his other home, Canaan. But it was difficult to draw from him any details about Hurwitz. I could picture Hurwitz with his bleached eyes and druggy's stare only as a mug shot. Hlungwane said that he had simply vanished, although another man had been found hanged: I could not make out the connection between the two events if there was one.

By the river there were some long-horned cattle and, as always, boys tending them. It seemed to me, walking along the river bank with this small, crazed man, that I hardly understood a thing about South Africa. It was the talent of white people – perhaps it was unavoidable if they wanted to proceed confidently in this strangeness – to discount completely the practices and beliefs of the native people. In the Suppression of Witchcraft Act any person who 'for gain pretends to use any supernatural power, witchcraft, sorcery, enchantment or conjuration' is committing a crime. And yet all South Africa's tribes employ traditional healers who are also able to produce potions for good luck, or to bring down enemies, and who are able to find hidden objects. But the truth is that I, and most white people, have no idea of the extent or influence of what the policeman had called superstition. It also seemed absurd to accuse people of superstition while building enormous, sky-vaulting churches to a God who apparently prescribed apartheid. Yet it was true that if Brandon Hurwitz were dead, it was interesting because he was a white boy who had become involved in this unfamiliar world.

Jackson told me that his given name, 'Idankane', meant little donkey, a reference to Palm Sunday. So here I was, walking beside the Letaba River with South Africa's most famous woodcarver, a Rasta called Little Donkey, trying to discover what had happened to a white boy perhaps ominously named Abel. Strangely, I found the experience exhilarating. When I was walking in Tanzania with a group of Masai I had the same sense that I was in another, parallel, universe.

In the art gallery catalogue there were some photographs and lavishly produced groundplans of Jackson Hlungwane's Canaan on the hill. He had built altars which were architecturally depicted and art works, including God's Television Aerial, which were graphically photographed. Jackson, because of his dispute with the chief, was unable to accompany us on the short journey to Canaan. Since the publication of the catalogue, Canaan had been devastated. There were the remains of the stone walls and one of the altars, but they had been vandalised and scattered in appropriately biblical fashion. God's television aerial, which had risen from a stone altar, lay on the ground, forlornly. Fortunately, one altar has been preserved in a museum in Johannesburg. Here the altars were rapidly losing whatever qualities had made them art.

Standing on the hill among the remains of the Little Donkey's altars and temples, looking down on the mix of round huts and shanties which makes up the homelands, the loudest noise I could hear was the laughing and shouting of children. It rose from the scratchy mealie fields and terracotta tracks and the piles of breeze blocks in a constant, unfettered melody of childhood. Children seem to have inherited these places. Perhaps, I thought, only children could make sense of the former homelands, places contrived out of racial fictions and invested with make-believe powers.

What constitutes art is a vexed question at the best of times. I pondered as I listened to the child-music whether there is a point where the intentions of the artist and the expectations of the audience meet, like lines on a graph. It seemed to me that Jackson Hlungwane's art and the purchasers of it in Johannesburg were on parallel but never intersecting lines.

Back at the New Jerusalem, Hlungwane was working on a small piece, now in a low chair with a fire burning near his scarred leg. His leg evidently has some residual affinity with fire. One of his disciples showed me the hut where he and Brandon Hurwitz had lived. He said that Hurwitz had simply vanished without taking his few possessions. He was puzzled. But I had the feeling that people knew what had happened to Hurwitz.

It was time to go. Hlungwane wanted to give me a gift of one of his smaller angels. I could pay for it if I wished. I declined to take it. We left the village, the disciples abandoning their attempt to sell their wares only reluctantly. Hlungwane was sitting by his fire, his mad smile undimmed.

Two days later our filming was over. As we drove back to Johannesburg to take Jon, the cameraman, to the airport, I suggested we pull off a forestry road for a picnic. There would be, I said, a stream and a waterfall nearby. There were both. The waterfall played into a clear pool, beside which grew a twenty-foot-high tree fern. This landscape, perfectly framed for a shampoo commercial of, say, a girl communing dreamily with nature while washing her hair, was something I remembered from my childhood: every small road in every forest in South Africa ends in one such, I thought. The woods were full of mushrooms. I photographed one and showed the photograph to Antonio Carluccio at his restaurant back in London. He confirmed that it was *Boletus edulis*, the cep, or porcini. In France neighbour has gone to war with neighbour over the cep. Maybe I would come back here one day and organise mushroom-picking, and ship the mushrooms to France and become incredibly rich while helping the locals. The air of South Africa is full of grand schemes and unjustifiable, but none the less enjoyable, optimism.

The absurd optimism and sense of well-being that whites, at least, experience in South Africa is probably essential to delay the onset of madness, or perhaps it is madness, a necessary form of dementia.

Chapter 12

A few months earlier, Lord Redesdale had taken me down the stairs of the House of Lords. The House of Lords, in common with the rest of the Palace of Westminster, looks like one of those ornate country houses in Ealing comedies with its spiky, gaudy, importunate decoration and its phoney historicity. On the way down Redesdale stopped to show me his family crest, in Victorian stained glass. He told me that his ancient family is the only one in the land to have two moles on its escutcheon. I wasn't entirely surprised because I had been under the impression that heraldry concerned lions rampant and unicorns couchant. It had never occurred to me that heroic moles could be part of the heraldic bestiary. These two moles, picked out by the weak sunlight diagonally across from each other, appeared to be not so much couchant as deceased, medieval roadkill. Redesdale explained that they were a reference to the two villages of Molesworth which make up the original grant of land from William the Conqueror to his family. A thousand years of history, and the two dead moles were still firmly propping up the family escutcheon.

Redesdale was a tall, amiable young man with the many years of his aristocratic lineage clearly etched on his face, a fact which suggests that Lysenko wasn't entirely wrong. He is the Liberal spokesman on foreign development in the House of Lords and the captain of the parliamentary rugby team, which was playing its own World Cup in Cape Town. Redesdale had included me in the party not to play rugby, but to take part in the seminars and social events, which were to include dinner with President Mandela. The time had arrived and I flew down to Cape Town. I was at school in Cape Town and the mountain still figures in my dreams, not always happily. From Bishops we could see it and, I thought, feel it looming over us. It is an extraordinary physical fact, rising almost sheer out of the city and more gently, but nonetheless spectacularly, above the suburb where Bishops is located. The mountain frightened me as a small boy, far from home. Its folds and crevasses changed colour and mood with the seasons. They were deeply wooded with that aromatic Cape flora, which meant nothing to me then, but whose strange perfume assails you as soon as you step out of the plane at the airport.

The mountain is Cape Town's cathedral, and for me it produced the same mixed feelings as a great cathedral of Europe does, feelings which are primitive and fearful at the same time. I never loved the mountain, as Capetonians do, but I can see now quite clearly why they do. Its landscape is on a heroic scale, inescapable from any point for miles around, affording now from the statue of Rhodes at the university a beautiful sight of False Bay and Table Bay, and then from the other side incomparable views of the Atlantic coast with its spectacular beaches and crashing waves. After all these years of living in Europe, I find the drive out of the city over Kloof Nek thrilling, almost implausibly idyllic. Down there, clinging to the narrow strip of flat land between the sea and the huge mountain, were once small villages; it was from one of these, Seapoint, that Antony Sher had come. It was a Friday evening as I pulled up outside the hotel where Redesdale and his colleagues were staying. The Seapoint Synagogue was receiving its congregation. I stopped awhile and watched them gather. They were elderly for the most part; perhaps some of them were Sher's relatives. The trousers were sharply cut and the bellies of the men quite prominent. The women wore suits mainly, although the few younger women were modishly dressed. They stood in knots, chatting, enjoying this perhaps more than the service itself. Jews in South Africa are in a curious position, as Nadine Gordimer had suggested. They left Europe at certain times for a new life and found themselves part of the empire. Their children became Anglophone South Africans, taught that the map was mainly red. But *their* children were brought up in a new era, the era of apartheid. Many emigrated to Britain and to North America, a Diaspora entered upon with quite different motives from other Jews.

The fragrant street ran down to the sea front where the waves were gentle and the giant kelp heaved and swayed, great submerged darkened forests. Like terrestrial forests, the kelp forests are full of invisible creatures. The Jews of Seapoint filed into the synagogue. It occurred to me that although Jews have a distinguished history in South Africa in opposing apartheid, in their worship they are spared any debate about the universality of belief, because their religion does not seek to be universal. It is the religion of the Jews, and so it affirms that religion is a cultural artefact.

At the hotel Redesdale had left me a note to say that the coach left early for Groot Constantia, where the dinner was taking place. This was five minutes from where I had set out, nearly an hour before. I drove back along the coast road and over the mountain at Hout Bay, along roads only half remembered, and eventually found Groot Constantia. I was deeply disturbed: this dinner with Mandela was going to reveal something to me and now, thanks to Redesdale's casualness with time, I was going to miss it. When I finally arrived, somewhat overwrought, I found the parliamentarians of many nations wandering cheerfully from the big house to the old wine cellars. It turned out that Mandela was unable to attend, and that the dinner was a buffet with everybody balancing plates awkwardly.

There were many speeches, from the Minister of Sports and Recreation, Steve Tshwete, a Robben Island internee, and Bantu Holomisa, a rugby-playing former Transkei general, now a minister, from Abe Williams, the Minister of Welfare and Population Development, and from the captains of the teams. Abe Williams, a large, jolly National Party member, formerly leader of a Coloured party, talked of the history and beauty of the Cape. Of course the Cape, and this elegant wine estate, speak most particularly of the four hundred and fifty years of white settlement. Williams asked, as Minister of Population Development, that the assembled teams take care, as he didn't want a population explosion. But the teams of parliamentarians were in jovial mood and some lost interest in the speeches long before the end, as though their rugby-playing personas had triumphed over their parliamentary personas. The truth was more mundane: many of them were not members of parliament at all, but the sons of members of parliament, researchers, hangers-on or, in the case of the House of Commons, a cook in the catering department. The speeches were informal and amusing: despite the absence of Mandela the occasion was imbued with a sense of significance that the genuine members of parliament clearly found invigorating.

It was raining heavily the next day, and the rugby ground for the event was right up above the city under the mountains, shrouded by cloud. The clouds poured over the flat part of the mountain in response to some atmospheric imperative, the flags of many nations were limp and 'Shosholoza' was played loudly from the clubhouse. The city and Table Bay below were only intermittently visible. The New Zealanders, huge and square, performed the *haka*. This tournament was obviously a very big event in New Zealand: the team members and all their retinue carried Air New Zealand bags. There was a lot of synchronised roaring. In fact all the teams conformed to national stereotype. The Irish were a strange mixture of shapes as if they were made out of human *objets trouvés*, knobbly knees, knotty little legs which poked palely out of large shorts, burgeoning Guinness bellies, unkempt Brendan Behan hair and an air of having just got out of bed.

It was the year of *Paddy Clarke*, and it sounded as if they had all been reading it. They all said things like 'that was a fine pont' and 'he's a grand player'. They lost, despite flummoxing the very physical New Zealanders with their elfin elusiveness. The British parliament, under the intermittently fierce but ultimately innocuous leadership of Lord Redesdale, was a mixture of hereditary and life peers, one or two MPs, an economics don from Trinity, Cambridge, a few PR men and the aforementioned Commons cook who was black, with a little top-knot of dreadlocks, a style which fascinated every black person he came into contact with. The physical South Africans were captained by Piet Koornhof, a National Party MP and son of a former leader of the NP in the Transvaal, who was later a founder of the Conservative Party. But Piet was of more outward-looking cast of mind. Abe Williams, president of the South African team, charged up and down the touchline like a rhino, accompanied by his private secretary, urging his team on, often in scabrous Afrikaans. General Bantu Holomisa, who described himself as an 'ex-dictator', played a thrusting game at centre. The South Africans won in the end, but not by much. The sun came out and the clouds lifted. We were directly beneath the towering cliffs of Table Mountain. In the bay below as the rain cleared, the water was still, stiller than I could ever remember it. Sitting out there, looking for all the world an easy swim from the mainland, was Robben Island. South Africa is crammed full of reminders of its recent past in the attachments and antipathies of landscape.

F.W. de Klerk came to see the second game. He seemed to have become a marmoreal effigy of himself, smooth, gleaming, borne along like a religious relic by his security men, who had watchful, wounded eyes and poor tailoring. It was raining again and a place was found for him in the clubhouse bar, overlooking the field. I found him at first sight a surprisingly sinister figure, despite the childish features. The doubts about how much he knew hung over him like a swarm of insects, I thought. Questions about the Third Force and its operations will plague him to his political grave.

To succeed in day-to-day politics is hard enough, but to drive through this entire revolution, this psychological volte-face, this – in Slabbert's words – deal, was surely beyond the powers of any one man. How had De Klerk done it? I looked at him and wondered what drove him. What inner knowledge. His wife Marike's expression on inauguration day would have been sufficient deterrent for most men. There must be something else, something more demonic about De Klerk underneath the pasteurised features. If there was, I could see no clues as to what it was.

I parted from my parliamentary chums, promising to return for the next matches a few days later, and set off for Newlands to see the preparation for the opening game of the World Cup. I remembered Newlands, one stop along the line from my school, as a small tin shed rugby ground. Now, among the old oaks beside the Liesbeeck River, a huge rugby stadium stood. For all that, this part of Cape Town seemed to have changed very little. Just down the road we used to have Sunday lunch with my grandmother, a doughty Yorkshirewoman; we had to dress up in our school uniform, having only just taken it off a few hours before. But the food at school was so appalling that I would have gladly dressed in a clown suit for Connie, her maid's, Sunday lunch. I remembered grape jelly with cream and my grandmother's admonitions about not diluting the gastric juices. The houses were, and are, from a suburban English catalogue of Edwardian times, but made less mean by the gardens and flowering trees and the exotic fragrances.

I wandered around Newlands pretending to be inspecting the facilities and chatted briefly to Morné Duplessis, the tall, slightly goofy-looking South African manager. Correspondents were gathering from all around the world. Journalists were accredited from countries where rugby had never been played. Confronted by this mob, the reception staff, young students, wore the stunned look of people who have just come out of a horror movie.

That evening I stayed with my mother out in Somerset

West and walked on the Helderberg in the morning, looking back across the Cape Flats to the great green liner of Table Mountain, apparently moored there with the sea on all sides. From here, high up on the hill, I could see the ever-increasing rows of small, square houses built on flattened sand dunes along the sweep of False Bay. The suburbs, Newlands, Rondebosch and Claremont, were unchanging, but these new cities, these regiments of tiny houses, told the story very graphically, of the new realities in South Africa. The sight troubled me: tens of thousands of these homes, tens more thousands of shacks, all jostling impatiently, not only with the beauty of the landscape, but with the hope of one nation. How could you have one nation, I thought, when hundreds of thousands, perhaps millions, were living in utter squalor, while others were living in Arcadia only a few miles away? *Et in Arcadia ego*: now it seemed that the sinister interpretation was the more real one. This could only lead to disaster.

And then I climbed higher up into a region of proteas and wild mushrooms, aromatic bushes alive with small birds, and I thought: perhaps it is possible to find a way of accommodating people and their demands. My judgements were changing rapidly and erratically.

I had been reading two books about South Africa, one by Mike Nicol and one by Allister Sparks. Nicol, among other interesting observations, said that South Africa had dropped the vocabulary of the struggle and that, I thought, was very heartening, if true. Sparks noted that Ronnie Kasrils's 'Leipzig option', the myth of direct mass action, which led to the invasion of the Ciskei, was a significant moment in the negotiations, bringing government and the ANC back to the table. Nadine Gordimer has made the point, in justifying Kasrils, that the attitude of those who have suffered torture and repression in South Africa 'differs almost beyond understanding from that of people who have not'. She says that in the current desire for testimony, South Africa will find the conditions for reflection. From that reflection, she implies, truth and understanding will come. Although I doubt if truth and understanding are possible, I can see that those who have suffered directly are of a different order. Torture, particularly, throws a plumbline into the unmeasurable depths of what it is to be human. And South African history is a skein of torture and murder and hatred which can never be unravelled.

The next day I was to see De Klerk again in a seminar in Stellenbosch organised for the parliamentarians (it was described as a 'parlementary seminar' in the official leaflet). The first speaker was Van Zyl Slabbert. Such is South Africa. He went through his routine about the settlement being 'deal-driven' but he also cautioned against over-optimism. The local elections of November 1995, then imminent, would decide if there was 'delivery' of legitimacy. At the moment, he said, the leaders of both communities were basking in legitimacy. But no leaders wanted the other side to take credit for achievements until the local elections were settled. He explained some of the difficulties: the tension between chiefs and younger leaders, the difficulty of acceptable policing ('you can't fabricate new people'), bureaucratic dysfunction, and the obstacles in the way of decent education. It was a thoughtful and practised speech, much appreciated by the parliamentarians, those, at least, free of hangovers.

Jay Naidoo, the dark ghost of South African politics, spoke next. He is an elegant, Ariel-like figure; the man is charged with making the reconstruction development programme work, and as a consequence considered to have the hottest seat in government. He seems to have moved from his beginnings as a trade union organiser to become an admirer of free capital movement and fiscal discipline, which was music to the ear of the parliamentarians. His speech was filled with predictions of growth and promises of investment by international companies. He said that there was a lack of skills in South Africa, like so much else, the legacy of apartheid. He wanted to avoid projects which appeared worthwhile, but became white elephants, as had happened in much of Africa. Development was being planned carefully and methodically. He hinted at the pressure he was under to grandstand; progress had apparently been slower than people expected, but there were real achievements. For example, four hundred thousand houses had been electrified. (I had seen some of this in Venda, electric cables looping up hills to clusters of huts.) He said that South Africa's two greatest assets were political stability and President Mandela. It wasn't the moment even to think how long either of these assets would last.

Lunch was served in the huge hall of the winery where the seminar was taking place. Sweeping down below were vineyards and rising behind them mountains, the Cape landscape, a settled, comfortable arrangement. F.W. de Klerk spoke after lunch. He said that while his relations with Mandela were correct and cordial, Mandela was his political enemy. He suggested strongly that he saw his role now as the maintenance of standards: the implication was that he would defend the rights and achievements of whites and anti-ANC groups, who of course now included the coloured population of this region in particular. He said that crime was the biggest problem the country faced, but there were others, the Inkatha and ANC power struggle, and recalcitrance of the trade unions. It was the speech of an opposition leader rather than a vice-presidential booster. He wanted the parliamentarians to be in no doubt that he commanded plenty of power and that he had his sticking point. He said, too, that he realised that South Africa would enjoy the world's attention only for a short time longer. And then he said that the rugby world represented the old friends 'who had stood by us in some way'. It was the Afrikaner view of the world, nakedly visible: the view that Afrikaners had stood for something valuable and worthwhile, and that certain people had recognised it, while urging negotiation and change. I wondered how welcome this little glimpse of De Klerk's feelings was to the politicians. The captain of the Irish team made a brilliant speech in presenting a shillelagh to De Klerk. After saying how fit and well De Klerk looked, he divulged that his team was short of one or two players, gone missing on romantic excursions or injured in combat, and invited De Klerk to play in the second row – against New Zealand in the final match.

After the speeches we parliamentarians, including a good proportion of impostors like me, were driven with outriders to the spiritual home of rugby in South Africa, the Danie Craven Stadium at Stellenbosch University, for an invitation game between a world team, captained by Nick Farr-Jones, and a South African A team, those who had not been selected for the World Cup squad. From the stand I could count fourteen rugby fields, like feudal strip farming, stretching into the distance in the lee of the mountains, the other side of the mountains in which I had walked the previous day. Danie Craven's grandson had been at school with me briefly, and that was thirty years ago. God knows what age Craven had been when he died recently. The little wooden house from which he ruled South African rugby was a shrine. I don't remember much about the match except that the South African A team looked remarkably large and raw-boned, and that they won easily. Farr-Jones came off early, hot and puffed, and gave interviews. Later I was to see him often in the stands as a commentator for the Australian Broadcasting Corporation.

We drove back through Stellenbosch. It is a beautiful town, with the old Cape Dutch houses opening directly on to the streets, lined with oak trees. It is a commonplace amongst whites in Africa that Africans produce nothing, that they have failed to leave any marks or monuments on the landscape, that their works are flimsy, made of straw and boughs and hides. You could see how such a view might have arisen; when the Dutch settlers who built this solid, reassuring town brought water and orchards and gardens with white low walls and soaring churches, they imported to the landscape a European beauty and sensibility, and in a way, I thought, it is these images of the properly-ordered society which are so compelling. It was to all this that De Klerk was referring: *we may have been wrong and racist, but here is our monu-*

ment, here is our achievement, it is my job to see that this is not, at best, ignored, or not at worst, brought to rubble. Let's remember the atrocities and lay them to rest, but let's also remember what was built.

Politics and landscape. Identity and landscape. Identity and culture.

But also, I think, there is something salutary in the casual observation I noticed in the catalogue at the African Arts exhibition: more masks and funerary objects have been eaten by termites than survive. When I walked briefly with the Masai family in Tanzania, I felt how lightly they rested on the earth, and I found this nomadic, unencumbered life attractive. South Africa now is looking at its roots and all the artefacts which are its beliefs, and trying to attribute value. You could see here in the pleasant streets and the broad, baked South African faces, that the philosophical shifts to come would not be easy.

The next day, after another round of parliamentary rugby, there was a dinner on board the SS *Outeniqua* in Table Bay for us parliamentarians. The view of a floodlit Table Mountain from the quayside was extraordinary. More than ever it looked like a cathedral, rising nearly three thousand feet sheer out of the city. Strangely, however, the party was down in the bowels of the ship. We might as well have been in a discount warehouse in Cleveland. As the party grew rowdier – the parliamentarians becoming more like rugby players every minute – speeches were made, but nobody seemed to be listening. The acoustics down in the hold were not good. Suddenly I heard a voice, 'Justin, man, how are you? Jesus, we used to get so fucking pissed.' It was the tall, elegant Essop Pahad, secretary of the Communist Party, my old university chum. His smaller and more rumpled brother Aziz, deputy foreign minister, was called over. I had last spoken to him in Charlotte Street in London. Once, since he had been back in South Africa, I had telephoned him, and he did not return my call. Now we had one of those conversations which middle-aged people so enjoy, reminding ourselves of our wild and irresponsible youth, and how much brandy, at 17/6d a bottle, we had been able to drink. Once we had taken a fire hose to a friend's flat after drinking this dreadful brandy, and I had been involved in the only fight of my life, which ended in a degrading and inconclusive brawl in a gutter.

But Thabo Mbeki managed, with the heavy-handed assistance of the South African team captain, to get our attention. He thanked us for helping South Africa. He told us that it was we who had brought about the changes in South Africa by our constant pressure. We had never failed to remind the world of our common humanity; the people of South Africa would never forget us. There were tears in my eyes, even though, of course, he did not intentionally include me in his encomiums. Mbeki worked the crowd like a master. We fell silent, stunned by our own achievements. And I realised that for the moment, anyway, South Africa had enormous symbolic weight for the whole world: it was the proof that democracy could triumph, that there is an irresistible momentum against tyranny and oppression. The idea of a free society never died completely in South Africa. But I thought, it's true, freedom for the wolves is death to the sheep. Down in the hold of this ship were the beneficiaries of both the old dispensation and the new. God, they looked happy, even ecstatic, here in the bowels of Afrikanerdom, right smack bang in the middle of a huge ship, something, until recently, as alien as a spacecraft. But out there, at New Brighton, at Crossroads on the Cape Flats, around Soweto, and in countless other dreadful places, they were living in shacks made up of bits of plastic sheeting and fertiliser bags and stray lengths of corrugated iron.

I'm afraid the reflective mood did not last: many hours later we were still partying in the bars of the waterfront. Where once there was one restaurant and the penny ferry, a rowing boat operated by an old man who had the complexion of a pickled walnut, now there were bars and restaurants and shopping arcades and scores of large people eating and drinking. The air was full of the smells of Lion Lager and grilled sausages, but also new, impertinent scents of fajitas and stir-fry and tequila.

Chapter 13

The proper rugby started the next day. Now it looks as though South Africa were ordained to win the tournament, but I and many hundreds of my fellow sports journalists – for that is what I had become with my media kit, pass and press box ticket – believed that England or Australia would play New Zealand in the final three weeks later.

I arrived early at the ground from the cottage where I had been staying. The roads around Newlands were already busy with flag-sellers and *boerewors*-grillers and amiable policemen. The favourite son of these humorous and self-deprecating Coloured people was Chester Williams; he was unable to play because of injury, but his face, slightly puffy as if he had had dental work, was on a thousand posters. The increasingly narcoleptic 'Shosholoza' was being played from within the ground. I had already found my way around the press centre, and discovered that I had no idea how to fax or e-mail my reports directly to the *Financial Times*. Anyway the *FT* had a proper rugby reporter; my job was to lend some colour and background, but still I pretended to be busy filing with pressing deadlines.

Filing: I loved the word. In fact my pieces were sent at leisure by fax, but the excitement of this kind of journalism, the massed ranks tap-tapping to a deadline, was intoxicating. The sports journalists, many of them ex-rugby-players whom I had once watched and admired on the field, were a little disappointing in person, but the foreign correspondents I found fascinating. They are people who cannot bear the constraints of domesticity; people who love hotels and fleeting acquaintance and good fellowship and chasing after the action. I could have gone that way myself, I thought. But I wonder if it is true: I find in fiction an order and a reality which is missing from journalism. As Nadine – I was, in my mind, on first-name terms with her by now – had said, nothing is as true as my fiction. I remembered Malcolm Muggeridge in his autobiography saying that when reporting the Russian grain harvest for the *Manchester Guardian*, he would often put the decimal point in the wrong place. It made no difference, record harvests of five thousand or five hundred thousand tons were approvingly reported by the *Guardian*. And in South Africa I had heard so much eager partiality for so long, that I thought now that my task was to focus on a few small stories, like a man with a microscope looking at cellular activity with a view to finding larger truths.

But there are no truths, only half truths.

We took our seats in the press box. Signing autographs near me was Chester Williams, in his role as Rugby Development Officer. Wherever he walked about the stand, the crowd called his name. The entertainment started with an influx of traditional dancers in skins, carrying shields, and a hundred or so gum-boot dancers, and then myriad members of Cape Town's Coon Carnival. (There had been some discussion about a more correct name, but it was dropped.) They were followed by schoolchildren of all colours. The pageant, when finally in place, proclaimed the family nature of South Africa, the importance of education, the glories of wine production and the uplifting nature of *ubuntu*. It was touching, colourful and, in that South African way, unmistakably self-congratulatory.

I have a entry in my notebook which suggests that long before the game I thought that South Africa were obliged to win. The pageantry – children dressed in national costume of the participating nations, balloons and doves cleaving to the heavens, songs by Brenda Fassie – continued until Nelson Mandela arrived to declare the World Cup open. Here he was, South Africa's national treasure, South Africa's greatest contribution to the world, the rock on which the new nation, with its many cultures, was to be built. I studied him closely through my binoculars. His face has become familiar in two guises, the stern, even autocratic politician, and the smiling, gentle man of the people. In his book – in part discredited – James Gregory, his jailer, tells of Mandela's ferocious stubbornness as well as his almost obsessive interest in family detail. Today Mandela was wearing a mixture of both faces. It produced a curious rictus at times, as the captains introduced him to the teams. These giant men emphasised how slender he is. But I was struck above all by the contrast between him and François Pienaar. In a war film Pienaar would be cast as the young Oberleutnant with a conscience. His face is planed; like the features of most people who take too much exercise, his skin has acquired a paper-thin delicacy. He reminded me of a ballet dancer after rehearsal. Mandela, I guessed, was enjoying meeting these hulking young Afrikaners, because he has a sense of irony. To see them lining up to meet their president was to him, who had had so many dealings with their kith and kin in the prison service, perhaps final proof that things had changed for ever. I watched the faces closely throughout. Mandela, whose eyes had seen so much of human weakness and cruelty, and behind the eyes I imagined an enormous reservoir of human knowledge. And Pienaar, a man born near Sharpeville, but two or three years after Mandela had been jailed, with so little behind the eyes. Young men playing rugby, dealing in simple truths, sustained by the knowledge of their own vigour and potency, see the world in a simple cartoon fashion.

Mandela is for Pienaar – I have spoken to him about the subject – in some way an endorsement of South Africa and South Africans. It's a cause for satisfaction among whites that Mandela is now so esteemed, as though, in some fashion, this reflects well on them. But I wondered, as I watched them in those few, charged minutes before the game, what the true relationship was. Did Mandela believe that those big, raw boys were capable of understanding the past? Already, with the pre-match pageant, you could see the way things were going: history and culture and differences were being subsumed into an entirely new mythology. And then, as Mandela waved amiably at the crowd, and the crowd chanted his name, I realised something: Mandela was intent on hijacking the World Cup. If a lot of farmers and policemen and students wanted to play rugby, and if the world wanted to report it and believe it, it must be clear that this was Mandela's World Cup, the rainbow nation's World Cup, not simply a pat on the back for the old regime, as De Klerk had inferred a few days before. And as we now know, Mandela did appropriate the World Cup and the whites were entirely won over. What have the whites been won over to? They don't know. They hope that it can be hidden in a welter of market economy jargon and stupefying reconstruction and development and, of course, in success on the sports field. In a sense, this blithe approach to existential matters may be the only one for South Africa. Existentialism itself has been described as staring into the abyss and making arrangements accordingly. South Africa has stared into the abyss for so long it has lost its fears. And Nelson Mandela, by endorsing the World Cup, seemed to me to be consciously acknowledging this idea of feel-good existentialism.

Although I have notes of the match, I have only two memories of any substance: the overweight Campese missing a tackle, and the sight of a farmer in a T-shirt reading 'Skaapnaai is Koning', which means 'Sheep-shagging is king'. The match, which South Africa won, propelled England and Australia together to see which would progress to the next round. In South Africa it was hailed as a triumph and a vindication; the truth was that Australia played, as they say in the sports columns, as if they had only to turn up to win. They had failed to appreciate that they were not playing a rugby team but an historic imperative. The Springboks were plumped up with this imperative, none more so than Van der Westhuizen and the captain, Pienaar, whose head would pop up from the scrum from time to time like a tank commander's from his turret.

The streets outside were seething with the exotic livery of the new South African flag. It suited face-painting very well, so that young South Africans looked like cockatiels. The feeling among those around the ground was that they were going all the way, a phrase that we journalists used frequently. At the press conference the Australian manager agreed that South Africa could go all the way. He was sacked soon after the tournament.

That evening I drove up to Bishopscourt to the British High Commissioner's residence for a drinks party. Lord Redesdale presented the ambassador with a polyester parliamentary rugby club tie, which he swore to cherish for ever. The grand house, not far from Archbishop Tutu's home, was done in that instantly recognisable, but hard to pin down, style of nineteen-fifties Surrey. It's a pleasant, comfortable style from a more confident era, long before the middle classes began to doubt their worth. It's always unmistakably present in old movies with Ian Carmichael or Richard Todd. I once stayed at the High Commissioner's house in Zambia and there it was; chintz, frills round the sofas, a table with *Country Life* and a few framed photographs, a piano and lamps on the walls with little shades. No doubt if we had had breakfast, there would have been kedgeree in a silver dish.

I set off for Durban the next day to see England play their first match. I had been writing my novel, *In Every Face I Meet*, which makes many references to Will Carling, the England captain, and the first person I met in the lift was Will Carling. We spoke briefly but he was, I thought, wary. Durban seemed to be remarkably empty. There were reports in the paper that the rugby tourist influx had not materialised. The Parade, stretching along the seafront, was crammed with vendors attempting without success to sell carved elephants and peanuts and fruit and Zulu beadwork. Although they had no custom, they sat in homely fashion, chatting. I walked down to the beach and tagged onto a police briefing, which was taking place behind a changing pavilion. The Indian officer was earnest and businesslike. He said that he had had orders that not a single tourist was to be mugged or injured. The policemen and women nodded, but the evening was so quiet and the tourists so few, it didn't appear that preventing mayhem was going to be a very difficult task. Down on the beach two Zulus had a fire going and they were alternately collecting sea water in bottles and then rushing into the sea to dunk themselves in the waves. I knew that Zulus believe in the magic power of the sea. As I do. In my case I believe it is good for the skin and the passages between the nose and the ears and so on. But like Lévi-Strauss, I don't distinguish between types of magic on the basis of rational and irrational. I walked down the beach, happy to feel the firm, abrasive sand welling up between my toes. Half an hour or so had gone by before I came back and the two Zulus were still immersing themselves before rushing back to their small fire. Out to sea a row of tankers lay at anchor.

The next morning in the hotel I kept bumping into the English team. Perhaps they were beginning to wonder who I was. Some of them were immense, men like Tim Rodber, Martin Bayfield and Martin Johnson; others like Brian Moore and Tony Underwood were surprisingly small. The first game against Argentina was scheduled for the afternoon. The players seemed to be edgy and impatient, already pacing the hotel, and they were due to spend another week or more here. Out to sea surfers had been bobbing since first light in their obsessive quest. I tried to telephone Rorke's Drift to arrange a stay at the lodge there. The woman on telephone inquiries had never heard of it. She offered Rocky's Drift. Then she wanted to talk about English music: 'We're so behind here, man, I want to go to England.' Eventually I found the number and booked myself in for the following night and took directions. It sounded wonderfully remote.

I can remember nothing of this match either without

referring to my notes, but I do remember the team bus setting off with the English players practising the art of looking focused, a new virtue in sport, which entails staring straight ahead and blotting out anything which passes through the field of vision.

'Smile, you glum bastards,' called one of the English supporters.

They were a rather dismal lot; the women were all overweight and they wore leggings; the men wore Fred Perry tennis shorts with about two millimetres of brown nylon sock peeping out of their trainers. They had all given the buffet breakfast a dreadful mauling. I do, however, remember a rainstorm falling on us in the open press box and the strange, almost palpable tropical light as the rain held up. My notes say that England laboured to win and that Victor Ubogo was far too fat. England did win quite easily in the end, but they appeared to be lacking fluency in victory. What should have been a very easy game did little for my confidence, often and rashly expressed, that England would win the tournament. Although I hardly remember the match, I remember the press conference. Some of the Argentinians appeared to come from the land-owning and polo-playing classes; some were stout, with flourishing moustaches Zapata-style. The Argentine captain said he believed they could have won. Nobody believed it.

The ritual of the press conference, as I was learning with fascination, was a strange one. The press sat facing empty seats until the players and the management arrived. Then they asked a few questions which seemed to be designed to establish a consensus about what sort of game it really was. Rob Andrew came out eating a sandwich, but surreptitiously as if, with his head bent double, we wouldn't be able to see it. Jack Rowell, the England manager, was quite candid: unless England played better they would be going home fast. I had my first inkling that England were lacking the physical exuberance that I thought would be needed for the job. It also seemed to me that touring could be very dull. The

England players were curiously inhibited and graceless. They needed, as Paul Ackford recommended, to lock themselves in a room and get drunk.

That evening I had dinner with Mike van Graan, one of the prime movers in the National Coalition for the Arts. I had met him briefly a year before. Now he was going to bring me up to date on the arts debate. It was coming to a climax the following month when a huge conference of all arts bodies was due to make proposals to the minister. Van Graan himself had been co-opted to advise the minister, as had his colleague in Johannesburg, Andries Oliphant, the local arts minister. First we talked about oil wrestling. A large tent near the rugby ground advertised oil wrestling. Van Graan said it was very popular and I would have liked to have time to see it. I wondered if it came into the ambit of the arts. With all the surfing and rugby and oil wrestling, the arts were competing for attention in a crowded market-place. Van Graan confirmed what Nadine Gordimer had told me, that the battle was largely won. The minister, although frequently contradicted by his deputy, Winnie Mandela, was very amenable to an independent arts council, which had been Van Graan's aim all along. Our conversation, in a hotel restaurant, somewhat empty and echoing, was interrupted by a man from Leeds at the next table. Like most Englishmen who have some familiarity with South Africa, he was eager to offer his broadly racist opinions, after the preamble that he had always been against apartheid, of course. It was difficult to stop him. We learned that England had changed, that South Africa had changed, and that he liked the seafood in Durban. This was said with such Dickensian smugness, as though he had given us some insight into life on the Indian Ocean, that I found it difficult to dislike him, a lonely businessman in a huge, empty hotel in Durban.

Van Graan had fought many battles. Already he and Oliphant had been called 'Dutchmen' by some of the cadres they had outflanked by their tireless efforts. I had been to a few meetings in South Africa where cultural issues were discussed, and found the speakers numbingly, achingly, boring when they weren't merely tendentious. Yet Van Graan had discovered that allowing everybody to talk and have a say, endlessly, produced results. After years of being ignored and being treated with contempt, this openness confused the more threadbare radicals who had been sustained by their hatreds and fired by their slogans. 'Yes, but what do you actually propose?' This was the question that eventually stopped them and allowed the more experienced and adept politicians to triumph. For thirty years South Africa had produced the politics of protest. What an army of insults, what a catalogue of grievances! Yet now people in the arts were being asked to suggest fair ways of spending government money. It required enormous psychological changes. Not everybody was ready. I heard Heraclitus quoted more than once: 'You can't step into the same river twice.'

But Van Graan seemed content with progress. Njabula Ndebele, now rector of a university in the far north, hovered over all our conversations. I had read some of his measured and sophisticated essays: he was, Mike confirmed, as chairman of the National Coalition for the Arts, wheeled on when required. I had tried to meet him and had many conversations with his Canadian secretary, but no time was ever found. He is another of those African figures, educated in the church school system, who seems to have landed in South Africa from exile, articulate, cosmopolitan and broadly liberal. I see them as the hope of South Africa, but I recognise in myself a tendency to rate highly the more Anglophone and Western leaders, which may well be self-deception.

I can't remember exactly what we ate, except that by South African standards it was expensive and over-elaborate in grand hotel tradition. But it was a pleasing conversation. I had taken sides, I realised, with the National Coalition against those who had initially backed an ANC-inspired forum on the arts. In the eyes of many people the ANC, it seemed, had become a political juggernaut, which must be diverted, pacified, tamed and teased, and to some extent wised-up. And Van Graan, who had made an art form of this mission, had actually been taken on by the minister as an adviser. He had offered to resign from the coalition but, on the Lyndon B. Johnson principle of sanitary arrangements in tents, had been asked to remain.

Only a year before he had been running an arts centre and festival of laughter on a shoestring: now, as was clear in some unmistakable ways, he had become a substantial figure. Isaac Bashevis Singer once wrote, 'When I was a child they called me a liar, now I am grown up they call me a writer.'

Chapter 14

I left Durban for Rorke's Drift the next morning in a hired car; after a few yards a huge lorry removed most of one side of the car while it was stationary at traffic lights ('robot' in South African). The driver of the lorry did not notice, so large was his truck. I had to report the incident at the police station. The sergeant, a Zulu, filled in the forms meticulously and courteously. Reluctantly the hire car people replaced the car which they had given me only a few minutes before. By destroying a car only fifty yards from their office, I had broken all records.

I set off again up the coast north of Durban through the sugar plantations which came right up to the road on the landward side, a sea of green with no life in it but rats and lethal spiders. On the coastal side of the road was a strip of forest which broke to reveal holiday homes and hotels at first, but quickly became less suburban. By the time I turned off for Zululand, this road had a frontier appearance with Indian villages, usually grouped around a store, and Zulu kraals appearing by the roadside. Looking at an old map, I see that it was the wagon trail north at the time of the Zulu War.

The rivers which flow into the Indian Ocean are seductive in their vowel-strewn Zulu. It is easy to imagine how the Zulu way of life and language so impressed itself on the British. In Denys Reitz's book *Commando*, about the Boer War, he confirms more than once that the Zulus favoured the British. It was strange that a war which in 1879 effectively destroyed the Zulu nation should have bound the Zulus and the British together. And one of the strangest events of the Zulu War was the death of the Prince Imperial, Louis Napoleon. It was across these sonorous rivers that his body was brought from the interior to be shipped to England. The *Illustrated London News* of the period devotes pages to the arrival of the body in a ship draped in black crêpe, the handing over to the French in exile and the funeral at Chislehurst. It was at least as big a disaster as the defeat at Isandhlwana, if the *Illustrated London News* is any indication. The Empress Eugénie, a Spanish noblewoman, never recovered from the death of her only son. The intervention of Queen Victoria was able but barely to prevent her from succumbing totally. If ever there is an object lesson about the precariousness of doubtful monarchies, these fly-by-night Bonapartes are it. Eugénie's husband, Napoleon III, spoke French with a German accent. He had bladder problems which troubled him painfully on horseback. The family was twice exiled before Napoleon III died in England, and Louis Napoleon, on whose elegant shoulders the hopes of the Bonapartists rested, was enrolled at Woolwich to learn to be a soldier. Queen Victoria specially favoured him and hoped he would marry her daughter Beatrice (after whom one of the Duchess of York's children is inauspiciously named). Louis Napoleon, the Prince Imperial, was, I guess, aware that his father had cut a somewhat old-world and occasionally ludicrous figure. Louis Napoleon wanted to earn the respect of his supporters in France. He wanted to be a modern monarch at a time when a powerful sense of the modern world was sweeping through France.

So he was determined to see some action in Zululand although he was not a commissioned officer and, obvious to all, was in a more than ambivalent position. Queen Victoria and the Duke of Cambridge consented reluctantly to his going, but instructed Lord Chelmsford that he was to be kept far away from danger. It was well known, apparently, that he was an impatient and reckless lad. (I see him as a French student on exchange at the staid House of Windsor, a menace to the girls and not to be trusted with the family car.) The events surrounding his death have been the subject of many debates. Lieutenant Carey, nominally in charge of the map-drawing party which was ambushed, had to carry the can, but as in all the politics of the middle Victorian period, one sees the emergence of thoroughly recognisable modern ways of thinking. The press and the army were deeply divided about Carey's guilt. What was clear, as Carey said in his defence, was that he would never have been charged with misbehaving in the face of the enemy had the prince been just another soldier. Other reports suggest that Carey was not even aware that the prince had been killed until he ran into a party led by General Wood and stopped long enough to count. A fact, often forgotten, is that three other men were killed; one, a black guide, is unnamed. The other two, troopers Abel and Rogers, have disappeared into anonymity. Rogers was still doing up his girth when the Zulus attacked; his horse bolted and he ran into a hut where he loaded his carbine and managed to fire just one shot before he was speared. Abel was killed by a bullet and fell from his horse. The prince had a party trick of vaulting on to his horse without using the stirrups but in this case a leather strap broke and he fell to the ground when his horse, Percy, bolted. He died sword in hand, some say assegai in hand, with fifteen stab wounds.

I have long thought that this incident demonstrates many interesting aspects of the colonial era. Behind this affair – and the death of the Prince Imperial was in military terms just a sideshow – I see the dawning understanding that the Zulus were not just suffering from 'the fantasies of helpless primitives', and I also see the realisation that different cultures were 'natural ways of conveying a coherent view of the world as it was seen and interpreted'. The problems of the attribution of value had started: in South Africa it has taken more than a hundred years to appreciate that culture is in any society just an attempt to fashion an accommodation with the world. One of the disturbing aspects of the cultural political debate in South Africa is in the fiercely partisan promotion of values, which has led at its most extreme to the Inkatha and ANC civil war in Natal. I wondered if it was not true that some of this conflict could be traced right back to the Buffalo River: to the north lay traditional Zululand, to the south, Natal, where a new and ultimately inescapable order had been instituted. Some aspects of history are blindingly obviously rooted in landscape; this, I guessed, was one as I headed up towards Greytown.

Greytown was completely still; it was like the setting for one of those apocalyptic movies that depict the only survivor emerging stunned, to discover that he is alone. True, it was a Sunday, but the stillness, the sheer lack of movement, was oppressive. The museum was closed but I was able to peer in the windows at the collection of memorabilia, which dated from all the wars in the area, the Zulu War of 1879 and the two Boer Wars of 1881 and 1899. During the Zulu War Greytown was considered to be in grave danger if the Zulu nation ever burst out of Zululand. So Rorke's Drift and Fugitive's Drift on the Buffalo River and Middle Drift on the Tugela were of enormous symbolic importance: they were both points of entry for the British army and the point of exit for the potentially rampant Zulu *impis*. The *impi* is a metonymy of Zulu life, the liquid, flowing, lethal hordes of Zulu warriors.

Fugitive's Drift, a few miles downstream from Rorke's Drift, is on the Natal side, a farm and nature reserve owned by David and Nicola Rattray. David Rattray is an authority on the Zulu War and conducts trips to the battlefield from the lodge they run. They own seventeen kilometres of the river. Beneath the lodge and its gaggle of cottages is the pathway down to the river, where the few survivors of Isandhlwana made their escape. After tea – there's always tea in Africa – I walked down to the river and chanced on some of the game, giraffe and blesbuck, which they have introduced on to their farm. I have seen many pictures of

Fugitive's Drift, with the rock in the middle of the river, to which a Lieutenant Higgins of the Natal Native contingent was clinging when Lieutenants Melville and Coghill plunged into the water with the colour. And there the famous rock was. Two women were washing clothes on the Zulu side, slapping them against the boulders, sending a little slick of blue soap downstream. Now the river was not very wide and the bank gently sloping, but when Coghill and Meville tried to cross it was in flood and hundreds of Zulus were throwing assegais at them or firing.

About a hundred yards from the drift is their grave; they made it to the Natal side but were killed, possibly by the supporters of a Natal chief. The evidence for this is that the bodies were not disembowelled, as happened on the other side of the river, where the warriors were obliged to wash their spears. The grave is decorated with a small cross donated by Sir Bartle Frere, the governor of Natal (and the eponym of Frere Road, where Nadine Gordimer lives). Melville and Coghill were both awarded the Victoria Cross, the first to be given posthumously. The sun was setting. The two Zulu women were talking loudly and cheerfully. The T.S. Eliot figures of the giraffes looked on awkwardly and it was impossible not to be caught up in the mythology.

The colour had floated down the river; it was retrieved a few days later by a young soldier-naturalist and was received with rejoicing and a hint of fetishism by the regiment. This young man was so interested in insects that he fell to his knees to examine a beetle while leading an attack against a Zulu chief. Today the colour hangs, tattered, in Brecon Cathedral. Back at the lodge around the fire, I thought that David Rattray had perhaps found the perfect life. Africa furnishes to some white people a sense of blessedness. I am as susceptible to this delusion as the next person; camping in Ngorogoro Crater, walking on the endless beach of Lamu, or just sitting around a fire of aromatic wood, as we were doing now. It was surprisingly cold. My fellow guests were a former ambassador and his lady, a potato farmer from

Hereford and his young family, and a retired couple who lived near Durban. We moved into the dining-room, a museum or perhaps a shrine, the walls hung with framed letters, shell cases, Zulu beadwork, bugles, shoulder and cap badges, diaries and certificates. Rattray speaks Zulu fluently. He has spent his life (he's not yet forty) immersing himself in the history of Zululand and the battles of the Zulu War. I signed up for the Isandhlwana tour the next morning. From the front of the lodge you could see the camel shape of the mountain, familiar from many illustrations of the Zulu War. Rattray said it was probably the best preserved battlefield in British military history. From here, with Zululand just across the river, it was possible both to see and to sense the deep divide, a philosophic and cultural divide between the new South Africa and the old. And in my cottage late at night, a log fire low in the grate, I wondered again how much of the brooding prickly recalcitrance of the Zulus could be traced to the mythology of the Zulu war. In defeat the Zulus enjoyed their finest hour.

We were up early, driving via Rorke's Drift and through a number of small towns into Zululand by the nearest bridge. On one side of the bridge was a white-owned farm, lush, calm and prosperous; immediately over the bridge in Zululand the grass appeared to have been subject to an attack by agent orange, with the wrecks of cars and small trucks ('bakkies') adding to the air of desolation. The rural tribal areas are disastrously short of purpose as well as of money. Goats and scavenging cattle are being driven round in ever-decreasing circles in search of ever-diminishing grazing; only the birthrate is flourishing. David Rattray played a tape on the Volkswagen bus's stereo to prepare us for the battlefield. It spoke of the Zulu regiments and their glory and the bravery and heroism on both sides, but as we were travelling – for at least an hour – I saw not grandeur and tradition, but a landscape and a people brought very low. Rattray said that during the Zulu War there were believed to be about three hundred thousand Zulus; there are now six million.

All the while the hill of Isandhlwana was visible, rotating

in the windscreen of the van like a gyroscope as we travelled down dusty roads. Eventually we approached it, from the same side that the British army with its miles of wagons and *matériel* had. On the other side of the hill the plain ran away eastwards into the apparently endless distance, towards Ulundi, from where, Chelmsford believed, the Zulu *impis* would arrive, if only he could get the blighters to stand and fight. Three years earlier, Colonel Custer had pronounced that his biggest problem would be to get the Sioux and Sitting Bull to stand and fight, with equally disastrous results. Manifest destiny came with unpleasant surprises.

Rattray took us on to the hill itself. Below were scattered cairns of white stones and crosses, memorials marking almost everything except the Zulu deaths. Rattray showed us that from the hill you would not have been able to see the thousands of Zulu approaching in a fold in the land, beyond the spot where the mission station now stands, and where the Zulu gathered to wait as Chelmsford, the camp inadequately protected, rode out towards Ulundi, a huge swathe of iridescence on the brown landscape. That is the simple truth of what happened: the Zulu overran the camp because Chelmsford made a number of erroneous assumptions and because he, like Custer, took little or no notice of what the indigenes were thinking. The assumption which prevailed until recently in South Africa was that what these people were thinking was barely worth consideration. The idea that they could have a coherent military strategy, or recognisable national and communal aims, was discounted. It is this disregard which is applied to the Inkatha Zulus by the 'progressive' forces which I believe inflames them today. Buthelezi has taken deep and lasting offence at the suggestion, first made by Elija Baraye of Cosatu in 1985, that he took the collaborationist and cowardly option in the years of apartheid. It is, sadly, true that Buthelezi used the apparatus of the South African state when it suited him.

Rattray's account of Isandhlwana is moving. He has talked for hundreds of hours with two of the sons of the Zulu commanders, one of whom, Mnandi Ngobese, almost incredibly, is still alive. His father was Mehlo-ka-Zulu, a name still revered in Zululand. Occasionally Rattray would stroke his Adam's apple with his fingers as he spoke, to relieve the stress of the ninety-minute oration. He told us where Lt Smith Dorien had stood. And about Colonel Durnford and the *donga* where he died wonderfully elated; and 'the strange dead calm' which hung over the battlefield after it was all over. He recreated the Zulu war cries of each horn of the buffalo, the traditional battle formation; he told us of the final desperate flight of the colour and of the scramble in the Buffalo River, with Melville trying to carry Coghill up the bank.

God knows what Chelmsford must have experienced when he returned from his magnificent foray out on to the open plains. In a way he was right: the Zulus did not stand and fight. There was probably nothing in his background to allow him to take into account – there was plenty of available advice – the military tactics of the Zulu. Lieutenant Smith Dorien was one of the few survivors of the engagement; he died in 1930 in a car crash outside Bath. This same Smith Dorien had chatted with the Prince Imperial just before the prince was killed.

From the hill we could see the run down to Fugitive's Drift, where these few survivors had tried to make their escape. Over to the west was Rorke's Drift, where the foolishness of Chelmsford's unprotected advance was made strikingly obvious, for there in the small mission buildings a few hundred men led by Lieutenants Bromhead and Chard repulsed thousands of Zulus by keeping their lines close. For all that, there seems to have been a strange reluctance by the Zulus to finish them off.

Oh Isandula! ever mournful name!
At once our glory and our lasting shame!

We came down from the hill. We had been sitting where the last survivor fell. As we drove back to the lodge, the long way, we were contemplative. I had a feeling that the grandeur, the folly, the melancholy of that day of 22 January in 1879 had leached out some of the human qualities of the Zulu and the British, so that we and they were curiously bereft of life and colour. There is something romantic and uplifting about battlefields for those who have never been in danger. Certainly the Zulu people never recovered from that day, although the final defeat was some months off.

I had little time, but I was keen to see the site of the Prince Imperial's death and so I set off, with David Rattray's directions, for the River Itshothoshi. It was not easy finding the spot, and I wondered what I was doing in the middle of Zululand as the afternoon drew in. Eventually I found a small grove of trees and a whitewashed dry stone wall, surrounding what could have been a family graveyard in Provence. Another simple stone cross, this one donated by Victoria, marks the spot. The inscription on the cross reads: *This cross is erected by Queen Victoria in affectionate remembrance of Napoleon Eugene Louis Jean Joseph Prince Imperial to mark the spot where, while assisting in a reconnaissance with the British troops on the 1st June 1879, he was attacked by a party of Zulus and fell with his face to the foe.* Behind the cross, tucked against the back wall, are two even more modest memorials. In fact so modest are they that they would not be conspicuous in the pets' cemetery in Kensington Gardens. Here are buried the troopers Abel and Rogers. These two are the Rosencrantz and Guildenstern of this affair, and I have been unable to find out anything about them apart from the manner of their deaths – one shot, one speared. Who were Bettington's horse, and why was one of the troopers in a colonial outfit a French-speaking Jerseyman, who suggested to the prince, '*Dépêchez-vous Monsieur, montez à cheval*'? Of the black guide also killed, there is no mention. This is in a long and enduring tradition a whites-only cemetery.

An elderly woman emerged from a hut nearby with the visitor's book. There were plenty of comments in French, comments which suggested a Bonapartist connection. I wrote '*incroyable de le voir*' in doubtful French and then wandered about the *copule* for some time.

In the contemporary reports of the incident the area is described as having thick reeds and vegetation. No more. The river and the *donga*, where the prince defended himself with an assegai plucked from his thigh, after giving up hope of running after his fast-disappearing companions and his bolting horse, is now completely open. It is hard to see how the Zulu could have crept up on the party, which was enjoying coffee, the prince and Lieutenant Carey in conversation. Carey had been sent to school in Paris and it is assumed that he spoke French fluently. But the grove of trees, planted on Eugénie's instructions – they looked like cypresses and yews – stands tall and green in this bare landscape. Behind the little cemetery, the hill slopes gently upwards for a mile or two. It was up this hill that Carey fled. When he stopped at the top and looked back, it was too late. In truth he showed very little curiosity about what might have happened to the prince, and it was this indifference which finally condemned him. The Duke of Cambridge thought he should have gone back; it would have been better still if he had got himself killed. Different times, different *Zeitgeist*.

That night, after a long drive, I was back in Johannesburg and went to Bellini, where I had a sandwich. It was a fat, New York sort of sandwich, stuffed with many slices of beef.

Chapter 15

The arts debate was coming to a head. After two years the arts workers and every interested body were convened in Pretoria to present their recommendations to the minister. Funding for the event had been provided by the Swedish government. There was a certain amount of tension. The officials from CSIR, the conference centre near Pretoria, were clearly not accustomed to this kind of exuberant influx: I heard them muttering about 'these people' and 'madhouses' in Afrikaans. Andries Oliphant was the chairman, proving, if proof were needed, that the Coalition for the Arts had won the day. He was smartly dressed to meet the minister, Ben Ngubane, who had so far failed to appear. I spotted Zeni Mandela, one of Mandela's daughters, and tried, unsuccessfully, to talk to her. Oliphant waited outside in the driveway.

Earlier I had walked around the grounds of the CSIR. It had clearly been something of a paradise for the officials of the institute, with tennis courts, bowling greens and barbecues scattered throughout the leafy estate. Guinea-fowl, obsessive creatures, rushed about. This was the Afrikaner *Heimat* made real. And now, of course, it was all being handed over to the new occupants. Or was it? I had a feeling then that the old South Africa hadn't quite got used to the idea that everyone was now an equal citizen. Yet in the conference centre coffee, biscuits, sandwiches and hospitality were being offered in abundance. Some of the arts workers from the outlying districts seemed to be in need of a square meal and were palming surplus sausage rolls and sandwiches as fast as they could.

Andries Oliphant still waited nervously outside. Eventually he decided to go back in. At that moment the minister arrived in a large BMW, nearly thirty minutes late. It is a strange fact that many people who achieve office in Africa become stout. Mandela's slimness can be seen as evidence of his singularity.

The conference started sedately, with speeches from the Swedish ambassador and the minister. But chaos set in the moment the minister left, after a measured and modest speech. How to proceed? A thousand people, each representing a different interest, began to shout. Andries Oliphant became moist in the face. It was clear that the document for discussion and appraisal had not been read. It was clear that this conference might go on for a few weeks or possibly for ever, if all the proposals had to be discussed in detail by all the delegates. Many delegates seemed to think the debate had just started; they didn't appear to understand that this was the final endorsement of the document. Some were not so much concerned about the unread document as about accommodation, food and reimbursement of taxi fares. The months of careful discussion, the long hours of patient drafting appeared to be unravelling. To add to the problems, the sophisticated sound system, designed for sober executives and academics and controlled by a computer, could not cope with this free-for-all. There was an unworthy attempt to pin the blame for the chaos on the white, Afrikaans officials, as though their sound system was a deliberate insult to the new, rowdy, free-thinking democracy. Help came from Mike van Graan. He proposed, from way back in the auditorium, that the assembly split into its component parts – theatre, dance, community arts, etcetera – to consider the document and its implications separately, before coming back the next day to vote it through. This proposal was accepted and the officials, now in danger of a breakdown, set about trying to find ten or so rooms in which to house the groups. Oliphant himself appeared to have suffered considerable stress. There is something satisfying in other people's discomfort, and the delegates spent a happy hour eating an early lunch and drinking coffee.

Eventually the session restarted. I attached myself to the performing arts. An elderly lady of eastern European origin, theatrically suited, requested more time for research. Her contention seemed to be that ballet was misunderstood and that it could be satisfactorily vindicated with a little more time. One or two of the delegates reacted angrily: she had missed the point entirely. This was not the beginning of the debate, but the end. The minister was to receive recommendations about funding of the arts and the setting up of arts councils. She sat down stunned. I imagined she had perhaps come to South Africa during the war to teach ballet and now found herself, for the second time in her life, cast out. Community dance groups and 'workshops', a depressing word, were of course hoping to get their hands on the money. The era of émigrés from obscure countries behind the Carpathians was past.

There have been many such small defeats in the past two years, but this one struck me as poignant. The old lady sat and trembled, fiddled with her handbag, tucked her silk scarf nervously into her collar and blinked, bewildered. She had discovered the nature of cultural relativism.

That night I had a different sort of assignment: Wales vs New Zealand at Ellis Park. I drove down there in my hired car and found parking in the garage of a block of flats, parking being sold by some alcoholic whites with strange tics. These flats dated from the fifties; their crumbling modernism now seemed to emphasise only the uncertain state of the area. I didn't haggle about the price of parking, twenty rand, because I thought these desperate Athol Fugard figures needed the money.

I joined the crowds walking down to the stadium uneasily.

The atmosphere was edgy. This may have been the headquarters of the World Cup, but there was something of Sarajevo about this place which I found disturbing, and a bristling aggression from the large white men ambling towards the stadium, which rose like the Coliseum out of the mean streets. The streets were full too with young New Zealanders and Welsh, their faces painted cheerfully.

Inside the stadium in the press box, I listened to the comments in Afrikaans of a group of beefy men about the press. It was full of hatred and anger, so different from the bonhomie of Newlands. I had played rugby against people like this when I was a student, a few times at Ellis Park itself, and I wondered how they were taking to the new South Africa. A New Zealand journalist sitting next to me said that the team was worried about Ieuan Evans, that he would turn Jonah Lomu around. When they came out on the field, the whole thing was apparently a mismatch. On the one side were chiselled, square, athletic-looking New Zealanders: on the other were lumpy, even tubby, Welsh. Lomu was huge, with such density of muscles and flesh that even then I feared for the English backs. At one point in the game Lomu picked up Mike Hall, the Welsh captain, and threw him aside. Mike Hall is the biggest Welsh back by some distance.

At the press conference afterwards Hall still looked shattered. Alec Evans, the manager, was calm. He said that Wales could have won the match on another day, a claim which no one believed, certainly not Mike Hall. But the truth was, the New Zealand team were from a different category. Only Robert Jones of the Welsh seemed to be playing the same game. Now there was no doubt in my mind that New Zealand would win the World Cup. I had seen Don Clark toe-punting the ball fifty yards in my extreme youth. He was a solid-looking chap, but these New Zealanders were angular, like a Cezanne with their square shoulders and sharp edges. Even their haircuts were geometric.

As I made my way back to my car I felt disoriented and lonely. I was losing interest in the rugby itself. All I heard was a cacophony of myth (if myths could shout) and it was deafening me. The Zulus, the culture, the rugby. As I struggled through the crowd I realised that I had lost the plot. This damn country where I was born; this cold, smoky air; this city poised on the edge of chaos: these poor whites selling parking, these farm-boy police with their dogs; these large men who ambled and shuddered down the streets; this broken skyline of rotten teeth; and this beery breath of xenophobia. It made me feel deeply uneasy. Perhaps I had become used to the European sense of aptness and the magnetic polarity which seems to hold everything in place. Here I could not for the moment see what the central physical principle was. The deal which Van Zyl Slabbert had talked of seemed to me a squalid thing, taking little account of humanity with all its richness and perverseness. It was a deal between two sorts of ideologues, who had fined their world view down to nearly meaningless platitudes. But I couldn't think, as I retrieved my car from the anxious, faded woman at the flats, what else could have been done.

My spirits lifted as I crested the hill past a round tower block, once a bohemian – in Gordimer's term – place for whites, now a no-go area inhabited by West African drug dealers, and raced down the other side, past the Fort where political figures had been held, and the university, so close, where liberalism had been kept alive, and down to Jan Smuts Avenue, and back to the northern suburbs where almost instantly the rawness of the city was forgotten.

I had arranged to go back to the city the next day, however, to have lunch at the Rand Club with the former chairman. In 1892, just a few years after the Gold Rush, Flora Shaw wrote of Johannesburg: 'There is luxury without order, sensual enjoyment without art, riches without refinement, display without dignity.' The Rand Club can be seen as the attempt by those who had become rich to institutionalise themselves and achieve some dignity. Cecil Rhodes himself chose the site in 1886, and the present building is the third. From the start the club was profoundly pro-Empire. It still seems to imagine there is cachet in the Annigoni portrait of the Queen and the bust of Cecil Rhodes. Anthony Sampson once wrote: 'The authentic gloom of Pall Mall is almost outdone by the morbid staircase of the Rand Club.' It was at the Rand Club that plans were laid to take over the Transvaal, and it was there that various members of the Reform Committee were arrested in January 1896, although the club's minutes mention neither the raid nor the arrests.

My father was something of an expert on the early history of Johannesburg, but the romance he described had seemed to me to be largely imaginary. The huge wealth that piled up, of course, had its own logic and that logic demanded that it should be secured from the grasp of the Boers. All these busts in funereal marble and portraits in heavy oil were a stage set on which the most nakedly capitalist war (and as Hannah Arendt has shown, one of the very few clear-cut examples of the type) was played. The Boer War may have been Milner's war ultimately, a war made out of typically complex motives, but here in Johannesburg patriotism was the only refuge of the scoundrel. Here, the war started effectively in 1895.

The club was far from full. My host told me that it was in decline. We inspected the memorabilia, which included a framed menu of a dinner for Rudyard Kipling ('Noisettes d'agneau à la Mowgli') and then took a lift operated by a uniformed but sulky attendant to the dining-room, which was large and sparsely attended. Lunch was avocado, hake, ostrich and apple pie. My host and I agreed that the ostrich was 'a gimmick'. After lunch we wandered around the private dining-rooms and looked at more memorabilia. Oh, the dinners! Oh, the patriotism! The implication of everything hung on the walls and displayed in cabinets was that British adventurism was in some way a noble endeavour, or at least a necessary endeavour. But more, I thought, it showed the powerful and real attraction of Empire, something which in Britain today has been discounted, as though it happened to deluded people who, fortunately, have left the stage. It was that notion of a beneficent red stain spreading across the map of the world – just as Chelmsford's magnificent forces had spread across the plains of Zululand – which helped this place, and so recently, into being. In the late seventies I met an old man in Swaziland who had been sent there by Baden-Powell himself to command the police post. His false teeth set up a dreadful rattling and sibilance as we talked, but his simple sense of duty to the Empire was undimmed seventy-eight years on.

The speed of history in the last few years in South Africa has been breathtaking. The myths are lagging behind, but I had a sudden insight prompted by this visit and by the arts debate: liberal constitutionalism seemed to be the only principle on which everyone could agree, however they were disposed temperamentally. Liberal democracy, variously interpreted of course, was rushing into the spaces vacated by the delusions of the past, including the delusions of the Communist Party (who had favoured a communist state based on the East German model as late as 1988), no less than the delusions of the devisers of apartheid. Liberal constitutionalism has been employed, successfully, by the coalition for the arts. I began to recover my sense of what was really going on, temporarily lost at Ellis Park. I saw now that a deal had been done, but the deal was based on the understanding that liberal constitutionalism was the only way to keep everybody on side, including the international investors and banks: they would provide the bread, while rugby and soccer provided the circuses. For a while the kaleidoscope of my impressions settled again.

I had dinner that evening with an American journalist, who told me that he and other correspondents had got drunk in Somalia and eaten sumptuously in the caravan of a US television network, while just outside the fence erected to protect themselves, the starving, the ostensible object of their visit, were dying. The juxtaposition of microwaved Maryland chicken and dying Somalis lent the occasion a macabre enjoyment. There was apparently a catharsis in this brutal exposure of the hypocrisy of famine reporting. Or perhaps, I thought, just another item from the catalogue of the perverseness of human nature.

When I got back home to the flat I had borrowed from a friend, I found a crisis. Doris, the maid, was in the flat with her very small girl, hiding from her Zulu boyfriend. The Zulu War had come, in a small way, to my living-room. She had tired of the boyfriend and wanted him out of the servant's quarters. She wanted me to go and talk to him. His honour demanded that he beat her up before he left. I didn't feel up to the task of mediating: more than that, I was disturbed by this assumption that a transient white person – me – was qualified for the role. I took her to her sister's house some miles away and in the morning paid the boyfriend to leave. I thought that the commercial nature of the transaction absolved me in some way from any of my doubts about getting involved. This is, of course, the specious appeal of the market economy: it appears to rule out tricky ethical considerations. As I left my front door later, which opened on to a small walled garden, I found a man standing by the bins eating a sponge cake with two hands. He showed no interest in me, and certainly no apprehension about being found eating from the rubbish, and continued to gorge himself. Very soon the whole Victoria sponge vanished.

I drove now to Pretoria to watch Scotland play France. I have, again, little recollection of the match itself, although I have noted that France won by three points, and that two people broke their arms on the hard ground. But I remember parking in a boys' high school and finding that the parking was supervised by large white men on horses while, of course, the actual work was done by black men. But what were they suggesting by this cavalry display? There is something fatally domineering in the make-up of the South African white male. If white men were beginning to fear for their position, I saw no sign of it personally. But certainly the *Boerestaat*, a landscape intended to enshrine Afrikaner male dominance, had become a subject of satire. Those whom the gods wish to destroy they first deride. To gallop around a rugby field and car park in overstuffed khaki trousers seemed to be to invite derision.

The sometimes absurd presumptions of male South Africans are far from a new discovery: Herman Charles Bosman in one of his sublime stories tells of a Boer woman giving her brother, who is going on commando during the Boer War, some advice: 'Remember, you're a white man. If there is any trouble with the British, send a kaffir to the front.' Surprisingly, even when General Constand Viljoen and others started the Volksfront, they made no attempt to encourage the police or the army to rebel. It seems that the South African male in general – and the Afrikaner especially – is held by contradictory forces in a more or less upright position. On the one hand he has in him a strongly felt assertiveness; on the other a submissive awareness of the incongruity of his situation. Van der Merwe, the hero of a thousand jokes, South Africa's best loved Afrikaner, is an archetype based on Bosmanesque shrewdness of observation. Van der Merwe may be stupid, crass and usually insensitive, but he is also strangely lovable and the possessor of Forrest-Gump-like human qualities. In politics, as is well known, Afrikaner men, but few women, have dominated almost every party at every phase of South Africa's history. Bram Fischer, the subject of Gordimer's *Burger's Daughter*, was himself the son of the attorney-general of the Orange Free State. There are many other examples of these polarities in Afrikaner families. The late and remarkable conversion of F.W. de Klerk can better be understood against the background of a left-inclined brother. In my own family there was a man who had been interned on St Helena and whose sister married my grandfather, an Australian with the Queensland Mounted Rifles.

I went to see Athol Fugard's *The Island* at the Market Theatre. This was a revival of the original production starring John Kani and Winston Ntshona. Nadine Gordimer had said that it is in these collaborative efforts that a new kind of culture had begun to emerge, and others have suggested that during the seventies and eighties the Market had served as a kind of rehearsal for the new South Africa. The programme made it clear that this was far from a Fugard solo, but a collaborative effort. John Kani is now the executive director of the Market. He and Winston Ntshona have achieved worldwide acclaim including honorary doctorates. In *The Island* they spend a good deal of time nearly naked. Their buttocks, from where I was sitting near the edge of the stage, loomed large and elderly. It is a very moving play, but like much South African theatre contains at its heart a sort of hectoring cunning, aimed to win over the audience. I wondered whether these endeavours were going to look less interesting now that the rehearsals for the new South Africa were over. That it was on the day the death penalty was abolished lent some cogency to my thoughts. Albie Sachs, whom a year before I had filmed in Johannesburg, was one of the judges of the Constitutional Court which abolished the death penalty. And it was Sachs who had provoked the most lively debate about the role of the arts in the new South Africa by suggesting that those engaged in the struggle should broaden their artistic horizons. In South Africa it seemed that wherever I turned I found connections, a spider's web of correspondences, but I wondered too at the way these connections seemed to lead a short distance to a very few people.

It was a particularly dark night. The area around the Market was quiet, with just the occasional glimpse of figures pressed into doorways or huddled on waste ground around fires. We, the audience, hurried to our cars. I had lost any sense of proportion about the extent of the dangers of Johannesburg at night. On the car radio I heard a respected journalist say that AIDS would soon infect twenty per cent of the population. Surely that could not be right? Despite the warnings against doing anything so foolish, I drove around the city. One street, not far from the headquarters of the Anglo-American Corporation, had been taken over by a group of men sitting around fires, lit in braziers made from oil drums. After watching *The Island*, itself somewhat

Beckettian, this scene appeared to me to be full of pathos. What were they hoping for? Where had they come from? And why, in the middle of the night, were they waiting in a place like this? If a picture was needed to capture the new South Africa, this was it: sombre, bistre figures around bonfires in the heart of the country's financial district, spectres at the feast, people with nothing to lose. I swung up towards Hillbrow. And here was another vision of South Africa: multiracial, lively, violent, the streets crowded, prostitutes on every corner, the scream of police cars tearing the air apart, scores of street vendors and music from apartments high above. *The Island* seemed remote by contrast, the violence and ill-treatment cocooned in theatricality; the past was obviously fading into incomprehensibility at high speed too. The radio said that there had been twenty thousand murders in the previous twelve months.

When I got home to the apartment where I was staying, an adobe arrangement which was due for redevelopment, I found Doris and her baby sheltering in the spare room. The Zulu, whom I had paid off so handsomely, was back.

Chapter 16

In the course of writing my novel *Masai Dreaming*, I had come to the conclusion that part of being human is the acceptance of ethical obligation. Even acceptance is too equivocal a word: inevitability is closer to the truth. If this is so, the arguments about ethics proceeding from a religious belief are simply an inversion of the facts.

Now I was beginning to see, too, that the moral-ethical component in the South African revolution, and South Africa's consequent importance to the western world, had similar ontological implications. South Africa was in a state of discourse with itself. The arts debate mirrored the political and constitutional debates. It was a debate about ethical obligation.

To the outside world South Africa had appeared, like Nazi Germany, to be an unpleasant product of western civilisation, the perversion of Christian and humanist values. How, for example, were intelligent Germans like Heidegger able to support national socialism unless they were giving their consent in some way to the horror, in the phrase of Emmanuel Levinas? White people generally were under suspicion of consenting in some way to the South African problem. The failure of ethical obligation, to which humans are periodically liable, must also proceed from the nature of humanness, just as surely as the innate ethicality. The historicists conclude from this that there are certain factors, economic and psychological or broadly historical, which will inevitably create the conditions for moral breakdown on a large scale.

In 1995 there was a sense of relief, despite the murders and the violence, that South Africa had rejoined the moral community. In the western world generally it was seen as a vindication of liberal values, accompanied by the satisfaction of believing that in the end these values were destined to prevail: we all knew that this would have to come to an end because it was against reason. But it also removed the guilt associated with being white while apartheid continued, a guilt which was not confined to South Africa. Some black South Africans were saying that there was more to this than a rehabilitation of the whites; the World Cup suggested otherwise.

I was preparing to interview Brian Moore, the England hooker, as I pondered these questions in Johannesburg. Rugby was providing the white population with a chance to show the world what they were made of, and they weren't talking just of muscle and sinew, but of a kind of moral fibre. François Pienaar, the South African captain, was coming to be seen as the exemplar of a kind of nobility which had been masked by apartheid. This led to another, more sinister, line of thought: the blacks themselves, wilfully or otherwise, had hindered the natural and ethical development of white South Africans. As one well-nourished banker put it to me, 'For forty years all our lives have been fucked up by living with the schvartzes.'

The English team were staying at the Sunnyside Park Hotel, Milner's headquarters after the occupation of the Transvaal. The great Randlord mansion, built just a few years before the Boer War, is now heavily camouflaged by the hotel décor and its extensions, but still recognisable with its baronial fireplaces and generous panelling. Huge members of the English team – the tall ones seemed to stick together – walked stiffly through the lounge where I waited for Brian Moore. When Moore arrived he was tense. Another member of the team, Rob Andrew, had suggested that touring could become tedious and I wondered if Moore was feeling the strain. His face was cut and nicked, as though he'd been careless with his razor. His abrasive nature is said to hide a deep intelligence, evidence for which is his partnership in a law firm.

He started our conversation brutally, cutting through my small talk impatiently: 'Let's get on with it, right?' Later I was told that he and his wife were in the process of separating at the time. But he talked interestingly about South Africa. He was aware that rugby had many resonances. The World Cup was, as he put it, 'more than just an event'. I asked him about tactics. He said that England could *go all the way*, he was sure of it, but I had seen New Zealand play, and now I was sure that they would win the tournament. I asked him how he expected England's relatively small backs to cope with the angular, almost cubist, Lomu. He said that Lomu would never get the ball. But first they had to beat Australia in Cape Town. The Australians had stood still tactically, in his judgement. Then he told me that the psyche of the English team was odd. It could have off days when nobody played with any commitment. And it seemed to me then that none of the team was more complex than he.

I left him already bristling at the next interviewer and made my way to see Van Zyl Slabbert. Slabbert is a fellow of All Souls, but he told me a joke about Van der Merwe. The crux of the joke involves a confusion in his mind between the words 'testicles' and 'test tickets'. Van der Merwe's preference is for test tickets if he has to make a choice. Slabbert told me that the research and development programme had become an incantation – 'om, om' – uttered in the face of all problems. He told me too of his falling-out with Breyten Breytenbach, now repaired. He had accused Breytenbach of appearing on the scene in South Africa periodically like a vulture to shit piously on honest endeavour. I wondered if the metaphor applied to me in some lesser way too. For I felt that there was quite a thin line of rationality and competence in South Africa, and four square in the middle of that line stood the bulky figure of Van Zyl Slabbert. People like me could easily become an irritant. If it was true, he showed no signs of it. I have known his wife, Jane, since my childhood. I was struck, as I sat in the drawing-room of their new house, by the sense that life here in South Africa was more vibrant than life in Britain. Cecil Rhodes had described life in England as petty, restrictive and parochial. At times I agreed with the sentiment, although I wondered if a romantic notion of landscape didn't play too great a part in that judgement.

I left the Slabberts reluctantly. I had a plane to catch to Cape Town, but my heart was not in it. Although the rugby was coming to a climax, I had lost interest in the tournament itself. I had a ticket for any game I wanted to see, sitting right on the half-way line in the press box, and yet I was preparing to go home after the next match whether England won or lost. There was too much rugby for me. It had lost its appeal, as a counterpoint to normal life. I had been to six or seven matches and seen a whole lot more on television and I no longer cared. But still, I felt I should see the game between England and Australia back at Newlands.

I went to stay with my mother again. She told me about her family, who lived around the town of Potchefstroom in the Transvaal. I remembered staying with them once as a small boy, in a farmhouse without electricity. Their lives seemed to have a Raymond Carver-like quality, of insecurity and minor triumph immediately followed by disaster. It pleased me to hear about failed farms and disappointing mineral rights. One distant cousin apparently held out for years in the mistaken belief that the gold reef took an undiscovered turn under his smallholding. Why had I never known this before? These were my ancestors too, and, had I cared, evidence that I had a home. It was too late to find them and re-acquaint myself. The very things I had been trying to get away from thirty years ago now seemed to me to be rich and interesting. My mother and I watched rugby, South Africa versus Western Samoa. It was a very hard match. Later there were accusations of racism. The rugby was coming thick and fast on the television: we talked about her family through two more matches.

The following day I drove into Cape Town. Outside the ground I fell into conversation with a Mr Ganief Dramat. I invited him into the press centre for a cup of coffee and we talked about the Cape. He was sixty-one, of Malay descent, and owned a business making clothes, mainly jeans, I think. His family had been moved under the Group Areas Act from the city to a Coloured suburb many years before. He told me that in the new South Africa there was a lack of realism about wages. He could not produce jeans as cheaply as the Chinese or the Zimbabweans. He was being priced out by the unions. But life had changed substantially; he had always been rather humble with his bank. When Mandela was installed, he took a more assertive line. Coloured people, he said, were not benefiting from affirmative action; they were caught in the middle again.

Indeed, during the election, despite the warnings of Dr Alan Boesak that Coloured people in the Western Cape would find themselves trapped in 'Hotnotsland' (Hottentot-country) if they voted for the National Party, a majority of them had voted for the very people who had removed them from the voters' roll and ejected them from District Six. As it turned out, the Coloured people were more strongly in favour of the National Party than whites. No amount of appeals to history could persuade them that their interest lay with the ANC.

Talking to the gentle and courteous Mr Dramat, I remembered Godfrey Moloi and his warnings. And I saw that South Africa was an even more intricate skein of loyalties and identities, fears and prejudices than I had imagined. Looking back a year to the inauguration, with its hopes that one nation would be forged out of this material, I realised, too, that the people of South Africa had achieved a certain unwanted distinction: in every issue in South Africa, something universal was at stake. South Africans now carry the burden of the world's expectation that they should meld into one nation peacefully. Mr Dramat and I parted. He had long been a rugby fan and had his season ticket and naturally he wanted to make his way to his seat in good time. I remembered in the past the Coloured sections of the crowd booing the Springboks and cheering the visiting team and having to suffer a hail of oranges and beer cans.

The match was extraordinarily exciting, with Rob Andrew kicking a drop goal at the death to win it. At the press conference afterwards, I asked my only question: Could England *go all the way*? I liked the phrase. Yes, said Will Carling, they could. He admitted to being absolutely drained. In my heart I knew they could never get past New Zealand. There were hundreds of journalists, perhaps even thousands, and I won the raffle for guessing the score correctly. My prize was a large bottle of whisky from the sponsors, Old Grouse. Over dinner with some rugby journalists I saw that my win had conferred some entirely phoney credibility; it seemed to confirm that I was not just from the arts section of life.

I drove home trying to follow the old road, which in turn followed the little railway line from the centre of town to my old school, every stop on the way still painfully familiar: Salt River, Woodstock, Mowbray . . . and so on to Rondebosch. Now virtually every street corner was patrolled by prostitutes. And always, up above, the mountain.

PART III

1996

Chapter 17

Port Elizabeth is South Africa's motortown. As the plane came in to land the coast looked wild and the motor town's industrialisation seemed to be no more than a ribbon along the edge of a vast continent, a piece of industrial band-aid, easily unpicked. Port Elizabeth for me is unfamiliar territory. As far as I could remember I had only visited it once before. Here the 1820 Settlers, the first sponsored immigrants, landed. The campanile which commemorates their arrival was visible from the air, looking remarkably like the tower over my local waterworks in London.

The airport is a rinky-dink little place. Although the town has a black mayor, Nceba Faku, nobody here had heard of the Truth and Reconciliation Commission, nor did they know how to find New Brighton, the township where it was conducting hearings. A black policeman made an attempt to explain to me, but gave up. Eventually I located New Brighton on a map, and set off in a hired car. I was already late for my meeting with Archbishop Tutu, the chairman of the commission, and paid insufficient attention to the map as one does when in a hurry. I soon discovered that the impression I had gained from the air of the extent of Port Elizabeth's industrialisation was mistaken when I quickly became lost in the apparently endless landscape of a giant Volkswagen plant. After a number of sweaty U-turns and half-understood briefings from work-seekers and aimless passers-by, of whom there seemed to be plenty, I found New Brighton. It was at first sight more prosperous than many townships I have visited, perhaps because of the proximity of the motor industry, but still it had its quota of foraging goats, cars on blocks and shanties of tin and plastic sheeting.

The Truth Commission was meeting in the Centenary Hall, a place of symbolic importance during the struggle. I was surprised to see thousands of people, scores of policeman and a couple of giant police Casspirs outside. As I struggled through the crowds to get in, I noticed a plaque on the exterior wall which said that Her Majesty, Queen Elizabeth II, had unveiled a commemorative plaque, possibly this very one, in 1995.

Tutu was having a brief lunch break, dressed from head to toe in episcopalian carmine. He was simultaneously clutching a chicken drumstick, congratulating the Indian caterer, shaking hands, processing around the room, and talking in that famous, excitable gabble. He laughs in bursts because he hasn't got time for the full effect. We were led through the crowd to a back office. Just as I readied my notebook, he said a brief prayer. I should have remembered: when I had met him in 1987 at Bishopscourt with David Steel, he had fallen to his knees before our discussion, causing even Steel, a son of the manse, a moment's confusion. But one of the things about Tutu which is most attractive is the directness of his faith. There is none of that mincing apologia which one has come to expect of Church of England clerics. Tutu makes belief seem natural, even inescapable, but also closely tied to political morality. At the time of our first meeting, he delivered an unmistakable reproach to Steel for having visited Chief Buthelezi. It was apparent to me then that the struggle conducted by the UDF on behalf of the ANC was at its height. There was a great deal of tension in the air and the constant fear of arrest. Tutu tried to suggest to us the magnitude and bitterness of what was going on. And it was then that I became aware for the first time of the impending struggle between the ANC and Inkatha. Port Elizabeth was the part of the country where the UDF's opposition was fiercest, and the repression most brutal.

The remit of the Truth and Reconcilation Commission is to discover the truth behind the human rights violations of the past thirty-three years, specifically up until 1993. It was set up by the Minister of Justice, Dullah Omar, with far-ranging legal powers. At the time it was first mooted he said that 'the objective [*sic*] of the exercise is not to conduct a witch-hunt or to haul violators of human rights before court to face charges. It is a necessary exercise to enable South Africans to come to terms with their past on a morally acceptable basis and to advance the cause of reconciliation.' It is clear from this that the commission is much more than a legal exercise. And Tutu has given the commission a decidedly sacramental function, probably nowhere sanctioned in South Africa's constitution. He stresses the importance of forgiveness and repentance, although there is no necessity for 'perpetrators' to express contrition; they are obliged only to make full disclosure. I had heard that under Tutu's chairmanship the quasi-religious procedure was causing concern in legal circles. I could imagine that witnesses, unaccompanied by lawyers, seeking to make explosive accusations, would cause upset to lawyers.

Tutu said that there was simply no time to have a fully legal investigation: it would tie up resources for years and probably achieve very little if the lawyers were involved at every turn. There was a pressing need for a healing. I asked him how the commission had come about. He said quite bluntly that it was a compromise, the result of the settlement between the ANC and the National Party. If during negotiations the ANC had demanded retribution against all the 'perpetrators' – a word I was to hear frequently in the next few days – there would have been no settlement. But, said Tutu, you could not have collective amnesia about the past: 'We were faced with amnesia, as those who facilely said let bygones be bygones were suggesting.' I asked what Mandela could have meant at his inauguration when he said, in

Afrikaans, 'What is past is past.' He had meant that there would be no revenge and no retribution. The Truth and Reconciliation Commission was not about retribution. The country had been traumatised; the events of the previous thirty years must be investigated and placed on the record. Mothers who had lost their sons in police custody, people whose families had been necklaced, men and women who had been tortured, could not simply let the matter rest. This demanded that the perpetrators come forward to explain what happened. They could ask for amnesty, and it would be granted if they were acting out of a political motive.

How had he come to be chairman of the commission? I asked. He said that he was due to retire from the Archbishopric in 1996, but was nominated by his fellow bishops for the commission, and felt that he could not refuse. His proposed sabbatical would have to be delayed. It is difficult to imagine Tutu on a sabbatical, but it is even more difficult to imagine how this commission could function without his moral authority. He is likely to be a busy man: the commission must report to the President within eighteen months.

A bodyguard watched me as we talked. His steady gaze was a reminder of the ever-present possibility of violence in South Africa, violence which still threatens the achievements of the past few years. I asked if Tutu thought violence and the consequent brutalisation had run too deep for a full national recovery. He said that they were just beginning to discover the depths of the depravity. He had thought that he knew what had gone on, but the hearings had been shocking. The callousness of the security forces was unbelievable. He had broken down that morning listening to a man in a wheelchair describe the torture he had suffered. When you heard people describing scraping pieces of brains and flesh off the wall, he said, and when you heard somebody describing seeing his son being killed, it was shattering. For all that he did not think that brutalisation had gone too deep; he felt that liberation had come in time. According to its terms of reference, the commission has three functions: the first is to note and investigate human rights violations in the period 1960 to 1993; the second is to recommend reparations for victims; and the third is to conduct amnesty hearings. The terms of reference make clear that there is a difference between random acts of violence and state-sponsored terror. Apartheid itself was a crime against humanity; there can be no equivalence made with the excesses of the liberation movements.

The political parties have been asked to make representations to the commission, explaining what their policies were and disclosing their own lapses, which Tutu said he regarded as of great importance. It is commonly believed that the National Party has the most explaining to do, and it is also believed that F.W. de Klerk must at least have been aware of violations in the period after Mandela's release, when what was described – with lipsmacking solemnity by the government – as 'black on black' violence escalated dramatically. More black people were killed in the period after Mandela's release than in the previous forty years. I had heard more than once that the De Klerk government thought that by promoting rivalries they would be able to form a coalition with Inkatha strong enough to win the election. The ANC maintains that there are no natural rivalries between black groups; all conflict was started by agents of the government. It is against this background of suspicion that the Truth and Reconciliation Commission is working. The danger, I imagined, was that quite a few roads would lead to De Klerk and it would be impossible to avoid turning this into a political issue, perhaps *the* political issue, as the next election approached, with disastrous consequences for national unity. (The government of national unity had already dissolved a few weeks before, reminding me of De Klerk's warning that he and Mandela were political enemies.)

But Tutu said it was only by going through this process that there could be forgiveness. 'If you don't know what it is you are supposed to forgive, how can you start? Truth is going to prevail over lies.' With this rousing cry, our interview ended; he was up and off, almost trotting through the crowds, small and plump in his cassock. I had the uncomfortable feeling, however, that he had not warmed to me, something which I would have liked.

The Centenary Hall is a large, airy social centre, like a university gym. The commissioners sat at a table at the front of the hall, facing the witness. Off to the side was a row of chairs where those who were to give evidence sat. And at the back was a room where witnesses were looked after and brought out to give evidence by two social workers, known as 'briefers', because they had been counselling the witnesses. As I went in to take my place, I saw that there was a large church candle, symbolising truth, burning on the stage facing the audience. It confirmed my impression that this was in part a religious experience. A surprisingly large majority of the policemen stationed around were young whites; they sat sprawled on chairs around the walls, or stood in little defensive groups. The hall itself was packed, and thousands of people had been refused entry on safety grounds. They may have been unaware of the Truth Commission at the airport but here in New Brighton it was clearly a matter of vital interest. This is South Africa today, a world where parallel existences are still being lived; where for most whites what is happening in the black community is important only in so far as it affects business confidence, investment and the rand. I wondered exactly what the audience was expecting from the commission. I doubted if it was just some sort of moral catharsis. I suspected it might be some form of payback.

The tension in the hall rose perceptibly as Dennis Meer, now the ANC police minister of the area and the boss of the policemen feigning nonchalance all around the perimeter of the hall, took the stand. Meer has a rather bushy, seventies, Jackson Five haircut and wears dark glasses. He was sworn in. The process was to become familiar over the next few days: the six commissioners sat at a table facing the witness, who could choose to be supported by members of his or her family on one side and by a briefer on the other, and then the witness would make a statement, sometimes with the aid of one of the commissioners.

Meer almost immediately named a Colonel Gideon Nieuwoudt as his chief tormentor during his period as a political activist. And now I could see why the lawyers were becoming exercised: Nieuwoudt had obtained an injunction from the Supreme Court forbidding mention of his name at the hearings, on the grounds that he had not been given due notice. But Meer had submitted no written statement in advance precisely because he did not want to be prevented from naming names. As far as he was concerned, the Truth and Reconciliation Commission was a long overdue opportunity to tell his story. By the end of the day, the Commission was facing a charge of contempt of court.

Meer's tale of the early and middle eighties was one of constant harassment, assault, torture, imprisonment and humiliation. He remembered with particular bitterness being stripped naked and having his genitals lifted for inspection with a police baton. His life became a cycle of torture and hospitalisation. On one occasion he was beaten for an hour and a half. Once he was almost suffocated. Once he was subjected to the infamous helicopter treatment. On another occasion he was offered the choice of being shot immediately or being taken to the house of a Reverend Maqina, apparently a collaborator, and being chopped into pieces there. He was driven around by an officer called Van Wijk in an attempt to discredit him. Meer drew laughter by saying that this Van Wijk had been promoted and was now in the VIP protection squad; on his visits to Bisho, Van Wijk was his bodyguard. The young policemen around the hall listened to the evidence without a flicker.

Meer was asked by Alex Boraine, the deputy chairman (and former associate of Van Zyl Slabbert), to repeat the names of the policemen who had been involved in his torture, and he was asked whether he had been able to trace them. Some were still in the service, some had disappeared. Boraine said that the chief investigator of the commission, who has a staff of forty, would investigate, and witnesses could be called. (I wondered where this would end.) Meer spoke movingly of the effects of torture; the psychological effects were permanent. Other witnesses were to say the same: torture brought about deep and irreversible changes, a fundamental melancholy. Boraine asked him if there was still torture going on in the police forces: there was, he said. From his personal experience he knew how helpless, how alone, prisoners were. He had instituted prison visits and greater openness, but, he said, at least torture was no longer policy.

It became clear towards the end of the day that Meer had started another storm: the Reverend Maqina, whom he named as a collaborator, had recently been made Port Elizabeth's citizen of the year by the ANC mayor, Nceba Faku. Maqina was invited to come and give his side of the story, with the threat of subpoena if he was unwilling, and that night the mayor stripped him of his award.

Now a succession of victims was brought gently to the stand to tell their stories. Wandile Appolis was blind. He had been shot by the police in 1981 at the age of twenty-one. Even as he was being treated in hospital he was humiliated and abused. He implied that in hospital something had been put in his eyes which blinded him. He was taken to Rooihel prison. Eventually he was released and he had been living with his mother ever since. He did not want to beg on the streets. Boraine asked him what he wanted from the commission. He wanted money for musical instruments for his music group; he was a keyboard player. Both Boraine and Tutu commended him for his courage and his unselfishness. Tutu reminded him of the success of Stevie Wonder, and said: 'South Africa will be a successful country because people like you who have nothing are still thinking about others. We thank you for your great humanity. In the end this new South Africa is going to succeed because we are going to help each other. We thank God for people like you.'

As Wandile Appolis was helped unsteadily out, everyone

in the hall cheered him and the tears flowed from my eyes. I wished that the people at the airport were here. Indeed I wished that a few more white people other than police and journalists were here. My doubts about the purpose of the Truth Commission had dissolved. Over the next few days I found myself constantly on the verge of tears, and at times unable to stop them. As Tutu had warned me, the callousness of the police was unspeakable, but there were acts of kindness and humanity in amongst the depravity. The name of Molly Blackburn, the human rights activist, was mentioned frequently, and one victim recalled a kind prison wardress, a Mrs Crouse, who had arranged to fetch a prescription given to her by the district surgeon, Wendy Orr. A later witness was to say that the police were particularly keen to play down the role of the white liberals. It seemed to me, as I listened, important that there had been white people who had acted with such courage and sympathy, but I was aware that there was something self-seeking in this, a clutching at straws not out of guilt, but as a confirmation of my belief that there was always a discernible and worthwhile liberal tradition in South Africa.

A middle-aged woman, Gladys Mqolo, described an awful Kafkaesque procedure as she tried to find her son Mbuyiselo Russia Maqolo who had not returned after reporting a robbery one day in 1986. She eventually found him in hospital, horribly injured, and handcuffed to the bed. When she went to visit him again he had been moved. Nobody would tell her where. Eventually the police dropped him back at her house, unconscious, 'his head was hanging', brain-damaged. When she asked the police why he was not in hospital, they said that his prison term was over, he was now her problem. He had never been tried. A day later they came for him again, saying there had been a mistake, his sentence was not complete. He was released eventually; both his release and re-arrest had been a mistake. Although he has been in a vegetative state for ten years, there have been no criminal charges against the police and no explanation has even been given for what had happened from the moment he entered the police station.

Tutu said that the members of the commission were proud to thank her. He promised that they would investigate. Then she said suddenly that the Black Sash, the white women's organisation, had helped her immeasurably in tracing her son when no one else would. She said that at the time her family was not popular even in their own community, although she did not say for what reason. I guessed it was because her husband, Chicken Kini Mqolo, was serving a sentence on Robben Island at the time. I saw two things: that the white liberals, despite criticism from many directions, had indeed come out of the struggle with some honour and that the antagonisms within the black community are deep.

The next witness, chosen from among the many applicants to demonstrate even-handedness, was the widow of a policeman who had been necklaced as a collaborator right in front of her. It is impossible to imagine what the sight of one's husband being burnt slowly and agonisingly to death in a rubber tyre full of petrol could be like. She said that she begged the comrades to kill her at the same time. They did not have enough petrol for two necklacings and she was driven around for a while as they tried to find more. Eventually she was released. She had taken refuge in a police compound in another town.

And so it went on all afternoon. A second witness named Colonel Nieuwoudt. Colonel Nieuwoudt appeared to have been everywhere, goading, directing, torturing. Without fail every witness said that any request for information about missing relatives or the location of bodies or of hospital treatment was greeted with contempt by the police. It seems that the police were unwilling to acknowledge their victims as fully human: as a consequence they found it difficult to believe that relatives could have a genuine interest in their welfare. It has been suggested many times, of course, that torture must be accompanied by dehumanising of its object. But I had been aware from a very early age, when I played in the river near our house and saw the police rounding up people without passes, that the police van and the cattle truck are not entirely dissimilar.

At the end of the day's proceedings, Tutu made a point of mentioning just how shocking – 'ghastly' was his word – the evidence of necklacing had been. Collaborators had been receiving their come-uppance, he said, but that policeman's fate was awful. (I thought the use of 'come-uppance' was significant. Underneath the cheerful bonhomie, Tutu, I think, shares some of the liberation movement's single-mindedness.) And now Tutu mentioned the legal action that was taking place. He said that they were trying to abide by the decision of the courts, but that it was difficult if witnesses did not give notice. Boraine then acknowledged that there had been great tension in the hall; he congratulated Tutu on his handling of the situation. Forgiveness, he said, is not easy. There were still enormous tensions in society at large, and they must never be swept under the carpet. Tutu chimed in; the audience, he said, recalled, as each witness spoke, what had happened to them. But, he said, it was incredible that they were able to laugh and respond to the evidence in the way they had. Tutu's role, I saw, was to insist on the innate goodness of the South African people and to insist on their redemption, whatever the evidence to the contrary.

That evening I walked on the beach and had an awful Mexican meal at a restaurant near my hotel. At the next table an Afrikaner was complaining to a black colleague in the motor industry of another colleague's intransigence. The black man listened patiently, although after what I had heard I was consumed by the urge to tell him to shut up and stop whining. I was tired after a long flight from London, and overwhelmed by the day's evidence. When I got back to my room, the phone rang and the reception said that a friend was on her way up to see me. A black prostitute, holding a bottle of beer and swaying gently, claimed she had met me earlier in the day and I had asked her to come to visit. With some difficulty I persuaded her to leave. Thirty-five years before I remembered my prep school housemaster bursting into tears after finding some childish graffiti suggesting he was having a sexual relationship with one of the maids. It was, he said, the worst thing you could accuse a white man of.

The next day Major-General Bantu Holomisa, a junior minister, came to the stand. I had last seen him the previous year playing a thrusting game at centre for the South African parliamentary team. From the start it was clear that he was here not so much to give evidence of human rights violations, as to settle scores and point the finger at De Klerk. He had been the chief minister of the Transkei, a post he assumed by *coup d'état*, and he wanted to justify what he had done, explain why he had supported the ANC, and tell how the National Party government had colluded in an attempt to overthrow him. He brandished 'top secret documents' which would show their involvement. He would give evidence that the ANC-led peaceful invasion of the nearby Ciskei, which resulted in a massacre by Ciskei troops, had also involved the National Party government, although they had denied responsibility. He too named Colonel Nieuwoudt as being behind the murder of Ciskei leader Charles Sebe. During a break I suggested to Alex Boraine that Holomisa might be making an attempt to use the commission for political purposes. Boraine said that the commission's job was to take note of and investigate his claims only in terms of human rights. But the cloud hanging over De Klerk, the suspicion that he knew a great deal about the black on black violence of the time, seemed to me to be darkening. Holomisa duly handed over his sixteen documents, which on inspection appear to be relatively routine.

For two more days I watched the witnesses come to the stand. While many were ANC activists or the parents of missing ANC activists, there were a couple of witnesses who spoke of atrocities committed by the comrades, and there were three white people, one a fireman who claimed that his department ignored or delayed calls from the townships during the eighties, resulting in many unnecessary deaths; another, a journalist who claimed that newspaper editors had colluded with the security police; and a woman whose two brothers had been murdered in the Transkei. The case against the men accused of the murder had been unreasonably delayed, she implied, for reasons of expedience. One of her brothers had been a Xhosa linguist and 'friend of the black people'. She ended her evidence by saying that she wished more white people had been there to see the wonderful work the commission was doing. The audience applauded. But I had the impression these witnesses had been included in the line-up largely for the sake of balance.

The proceedings took a farcical turn the next day when Mkhuseli Jack, a well-known ANC activist during the eighties, was asked, as required by the policeman's lawyers, if he was proposing to name Colonel Nieuwoudt. Jack, who proved to be the most articulate and sophisticated of witnesses, said that seventy per cent of his evidence concerned Nieuwoudt, but that as he respected the constitution and the rule of law and the standing of the country, he would refer to him only as 'Mr X' or 'The man we cannot name'. The audience laughed. His evidence was both in English and in Xhosa, and the audience appeared to be able to follow either language without difficulty. Only the journalists and police were supplied with headsets, although one of the commissioners, who had spent thirty years in America, said that her Xhosa was rusty. Before giving his evidence, Jack said that he had recently returned from London University, where he had studied business; he was now, he said with a deprecating smile, trying to be a businessman.

His evidence was harrowing, and much of it did indeed concern Mr X. He described how active and omnipresent Mr X was. Mr X was clearly a man who had found his vocation. By this stage I had begun to recognise the names not only of individual policemen, but of the prisons and the hospitals where Jack often found himself. Later a black doctor was to say that some of the doctors simply certified prisoners as ready for more torture, although one of the provincial doctors at the time, Wendy Orr, had courageously made public evidence of torture by the Special Branch. (She is now a member of the commission.) Jack said she had burst into tears when she examined him after one beating.

He also told of how Mr X tried to discredit him, by driving him ostentatiously around the townships in a car, his handcuffs hidden beneath an orange sack, offering him cigarettes, pretending to be friendly. Jack said he was lucky; other comrades had been killed as informers for less. The policemen were angry with him on one occasion because they had heard that he had said in a speech in Cape Town that they were worse than Ivan the Terrible and as bad as the Gestapo. In fact they were so angry at this slur that they had beaten him up. Jack, too, said how humiliating the torture was, as he described being manacled, beaten, and hung between two tables. 'What hurts the most,' he said, 'is the psychological damage.' As Bruno Bettelheim wrote of his experiences in Büchenwald, surviving torture is 'an existential predicament which does not permit of any solution'. These witnesses had seen the dark side of human nature, and their testimony, I thought, was of the most profound importance to South Africa's understanding of its past, although I wasn't sure precisely what that entailed. Some of South Africa's past seems literally incomprehensible, or lost.

The lunch break saw an invasion. Two thousand schoolchildren and students from the township invaded the hall; their leaders seized the microphones and harangued the crowd about a court order preventing one of the witnesses from speaking. Her son, Siphiwo Mtsimkulu, who disappeared in 1982, had been a student leader in New Brighton. It was an unsettling demonstration of mob power. Mkhuseli Jack, fresh from giving evidence, was outraged: Nelson Mandela was that very day in Germany trying to raise money for South Africa. The constitution was now their constitution;

they could not go against it; they were contributing to the impression that there was anarchy in South Africa. He and his comrades had fought for the rule of law. Over the break a deal was struck: the witness would give evidence another day when due notice had been given to the policemen who were to be named; the commission would return to Port Elizabeth specifically for that purpose. The mayor confirmed on behalf of local people that they would accept the deal, although he issued a warning about what would happen if the witness's evidence was not heard. The witness herself confirmed that she had no wish to defy the law; it was now their law, even if white policemen who had never taken any notice of it previously were taking advantage of it. The crisis had passed. In the initial scrum, into which I had naturally pushed myself eagerly, I had been warned that shooting could break out, although it seemed very unlikely to me. Archbishop Tutu was not there, but the Reverend Finca, the chairman for the day, managed to impose something of the liturgical calm which had reigned earlier. The schoolchildren and students gradually left the hall.

Now a succession of mothers came to give evidence. They were mostly prematurely elderly, simply dressed, at first hesitant, but soon buoyed up with the opportunity to tell their stories. They were treated with the utmost courtesy and dignity by the commission. Many had had the awful experience of being taken to the morgue to identify their sons. Few of them knew exactly what had happened. There were no court cases, no investigations and no compensation paid. One woman wanted to know if her son had been taken away for training by the ANC as she had heard: he had never returned. Another told of looking in black rubbish bags dumped by a river and finding the decomposed body of another man, a friend of her son. Three women named a farmer who was said to have killed their sons. One of them said she would like a memorial to be erected by the commission. Another woman, whose husband, a councillor, had been killed as a collaborator in the most brutal fashion, wanted to know what they had done to deserve it. A later witness, an ANC organiser, said, without wishing to minimise the woman's plight, that her husband had firebombed his house in collaboration with the police; his brother had burned to death. And so it went on. I remembered Hannah Arendt's phrase, 'the banality of evil'. Evil, it was very obvious, flourished where it was trivialised.

That evening I drove around Port Elizabeth aimlessly. The city itself is almost eerily quiet at night. Up the hill from the port is an area of Victorian houses and a theatre, the only functioning Victorian theatre in the country, which I explored briefly. I wondered how the commission was going to investigate the tens of thousands of deaths that could not be directly attributed to the security forces. And I wondered if the whole process, despite Archbishop Tutu's assurances that truth would prevail over lies, would not simply uncover more and more evil, more and more violence, and more and more evidence of the depravity of South Africa. One of the commissioners had explained to me that witnesses were chosen with some symbolic intent from the many applicants, which made me wonder how the relative importance of symbols was being evaluated. At the same time I could see clearly how necessary the Truth and Reconciliation Commission was, even if it could never achieve the proclaimed grand aim of healing the country, at least for placing on the record a fuller account of what apartheid involved. Some whites have an understandable inclination to minimise what went on in the name of apartheid. After the Truth and Reconciliation Commission it will no longer be possible for anyone to be under any illusions.

As I left Port Elizabeth at the end of the week, I remembered above all the mothers, and their tears of gratitude as, at last, someone in power listened to them. Their tears were like rainfall on dry ground. Now I thought I understood Milan Kundera's phrase, that the struggle of man against power is the struggle of memory against oblivion.

On the plane I read that the Lebanese chargé d'affaires,

Charbel Stephan, was proposing to return home after an armed robbery at his residence in Johannesburg. He felt safer in Beirut.

Conclusion

Mountains are the beginning and end of all scenery, wrote Ruskin in 1856.

I am writing this and looking out of the window of the Hotel Dahu in Argentière, Chamonix, up at the glacier, aware now of the seductions a sense of place – scenery – can promise. Ruskin made many trips to Chamonix and found in the glaciers and mountain peaks his 'blessed entrance into life'. Ruskin thought of mountains as natural cathedrals, ante-chambers of something more real. I realise that I have been susceptible to this idea; in my novel *Interior*, for example, the mountains are the last and significant resting-place of the remains of the narrator's father. But even a cursory knowledge of ethnography suggests that mountains appeal to almost all cultures in some deep fashion. Bad luck, in Ruskin's opinion, on those who live in flat countries.

Perhaps because of the sense, often full of foreboding, that I had of the mountain hanging over me as a schoolboy, my feelings about mountains are more equivocal than Ruskin's. In the past three years I have also come to see that while many of my feelings about South Africa were more complex than I had imagined, many of my judgements were, to put it bluntly, wrong. I have found South Africa revealing to me what must always have been there, but somehow out of sight, in a way that has been both exhilarating and disturbing. As a boy I used to find the turbulence of the clouds continually pouring over the mountain and then lifting strangely unsettling. I have the same feeling about South Africa today.

The mountains around here claim many lives each year. I know someone whose husband was killed when a huge wall of the glacier came away unexpectedly. The little churchyard commemorates more than one climber who died here. Yesterday I tore a calf muscle on the mountain. The man who melts the Reblochon cheese for the raclette gave me three chestnuts to put in my pocket, a surefire remedy. Note well, not cultivated chestnuts, but marrons. And, of course, you must believe. I have them in my pocket in full expectation of recovery. The view of the mountain – the sun is shining – from here is almost perfect. I can't see the not-so-modern flats where French trade unionists stay on their subsidised leave, nor the Yeti with its out-of-date games machines. The spire of the church – Alpine baroque, a style imported from Austria – framed between the Mairie and the Post Office, thrusts up into the frame, just clipping the bottom of the glacier. The glacier itself is gleaming blue in places, giving some indication of the vast depth of the cataract of ice, nudging downwards to its own destruction in a natural process which Ruskin found thrilling. This glacier groans and sometimes roars. In summer huge chunks and boulders of ice fall from the slowly advancing ice cliff. Further down the valley a few years ago a glacier raced down the hill, bulldozing some chalets, and stopped just short of the Novotel, a huge wall of ice full of trees and real boulders which took two years to melt. The Novotel is still there.

The strange thing is, until Ruskin and the others came along, the locals had not realised just how significant their mountains were in the global scheme of things.

A few days ago, I heard that Brandon Hurwitz was not dead. I could have found out earlier, but I wanted to wait until I was finished writing. He had not been used for medicine, nor been murdered by the local chief, nor thrown to a white crocodile. He had wandered off, just as Smiley Bezuidenhout had said. (I regret my unworthy smirks in the police station.) Now I am about to speak to Brandon's mother. I have obtained her phone number. I am dialling. The phone is ringing.

'Hello.'

'Hello, is that Mrs Hurwitz?'

'Yes.' (Prolonged: 'Ye-ee-es?')

'I was given your phone number by Rick Burnett.'

'I beg yours?'

'It's about your son Brandon.'

'Oh yes?'

Her voice is curiously fluted, a Cape accent. I explain that I am the person who was making a film about Jackson Hlungwane when I heard about her son. (It seems sensible to keep it simple. I have no clear idea of what I am hoping to hear.)

She says that at first she was not too worried when Brandon disappeared, because he had often wandered off. But then a freelance writer contacted her – he was black – saying that he had information that Brandon's body parts were 'in the underground fridge belonging to this chief'. She was so worried, she says, that she contacted a medium, a psychic lady, who told her that Brandon was far away but safe. Mrs Hurwitz says that she was reassured and took to wearing an African bangle around her wrist.

'How did you find out where he was?'

A church group, on a choral singing expedition to Zambia, heard about him and made inquiries. He had been arrested near the Tanzanian border wearing only his father's tuxedo. The police had found 'a teaspoon' of marijuana on him and jailed him. He had no papers and identified himself only as Abel, the name Hlungwane had given him. The jail was some way from the capital and he was forgotten; no attempt was made by the Zambian police to find out anything more about him. Eventually the church group contacted her, she sent some money, and Brandon was released.

Mrs Hurwitz thinks it is a wonderful story, a miracle, and she sees herself in a film with somebody playing Smiley

Bezuidenhout, 'who became my Mickey Spillane'. Brandon is, she says, a lovely person. He comes from a loving home, but he has always liked the ethnic life.

I tell her that I would like to speak to Brandon one day.

'No problem. He's right here. Brandon, Brandon, go to the top phone, a man wants to speak to you.'

'Hello.'

I explain briefly who I am, and Brandon seems happy enough with the explanation.

He tells me that he was in jail for eight or nine months. He has a distinct African accent. I ask him about Hlungwane. He says he has been wanting to go back. He was doing woodcarving and sculpting, with religious significance. He was staying with a Shangaan girl. ('Staying with' in South African can mean 'living with'.) I ask him why he decided to leave without telling anyone.

'It was like I was just wanting to explore, but not knowing what I was looking for. A force was pulling me. It was all going very well until I was arrested.'

I try to imagine what it is like to walk through Zimbabwe and most of Zambia in a dinner jacket, without papers. It's a journey of at least a thousand miles, in a straight line. I ask him if he was worried when he was jailed.

He was not worried at first. Eventually he was transferred to another prison nearer Lusaka. I ask him about Rastafarianism. He became a Rasta without realising it; his 'dreads' apparently coming before any vocation. It took him some time to realise that Hlungwane was also 'carrying dreads'. When Hlungwane explained his beliefs, he was struck by the revelation that he had been a self-taught Rasta all along. Hlungwane showed him how to use the traditional adze and inspired him in his further studies.

I ask him about traditional beliefs among the tribes around Hlungwane's home. He says that it is believed that if you wear the skin of a crocodile you are invisible. He suggests that he might have been invisible on his long walk because he wore a strip of crocodile skin. He will go back one day and resume his work there. I tell him that Hlungwane's altars have been destroyed. He finds this very sad. He hasn't heard this before. Although he says he will go back, I imagine that he has lost touch with his former life and self.

I ask if I may speak to him again at some later date, and he is perfectly agreeable: 'Sure. Why not?'

Outside the window, the glacier has begun to glisten, which it does when the sun is at its hottest. In truth, the process is no more than ceaseless, pointless chemistry. My thoughts are, however, far from Ruskin and his scenery now. I am with Abel who liked the ethnic life and walked all those miles in search of revelation. Something was drawing him. And I remember his mentor, Jackson Hlungwane, the Little Donkey, South Africa's premier woodcarver, himself a Rasta, looking forward to a time when there will be no more black and white. As he tells me this he is conjuring angel features out of logs, features which Rick Burnett says are Blakean. And Brandon's mother believes that this story has the makings of a great movie, with Smiley Bezuidenhout as Bogart and herself as Bacall. She believes that Africa is all the rage now. There are so many correspondences in all this, too many to tie up neatly.

I take this story to be another example of the strangeness, the newly discovered property, of South Africa today. What Nadine Gordimer called the interregnum has indeed ended. But the point about the end of an interregnum is that something familiar returns. The single, and only, attractive aspect of apartheid is that it was very easy to understand: it was clearly codified; it was obviously unjust; and it was mind-numbingly stupid. All political endeavour for fifty years was directed either to destroying it or to defending it. All social discourse revolved on its axis. Now there are no certainties. When apartheid died, there were found to be codicils in the will: South Africa is still trying to decipher their meaning. This is the legacy of apartheid.

* * *

More than two years have gone since the elections which brought Nelson Mandela into his kingdom. He is doing his best to stand proxy for all of us. *Ich bin du*, *Wenn Ich Ich bin*. ('I am you when I am I.' Paul Celan.)

This transfiguration, like all good myths, will extend beyond death.

Out of the window I can hear the glacier rumble. It reminds me how far I am from home.